THE HISTORY OF TREK

Designed and Edited by Hal Schuster
with assistance from David Lessnick

JAMES VAN HISE writes about film, television and comic book history. He has written numerous books on these subjects, including BAT-MANIA, HORROR IN THE 80S, THE TREK CREW BOOK, STEPHEN KING & CLIVE BARKER: THE ILLUSTRATED GUIDE TO THE MASTERS OF THE MACABRE and HOW TO DRAW ART FOR COMIC BOOKS: LESSONS FROM THE MASTERS. He is the publisher of MIDNIGHT GRAFFITI, in which he has run previously unpublished stories by Stephen King and Harlan Ellison. Van Hise resides in San Diego along with his wife, horses and various other animals.

THE HISTORY OF
TREK

By James Van Hise

Books for the entertainment buyer

PIONEER

Library of Congress Cataloging-in-Publication Data

    1.   The History of Trek (popular culture)

 I. Title

Published by Pioneer Books, Inc., 5715 N. Balsam Rd., Las Vegas, NV, 89130.

This publication is not licenced by, nor is Pioneer Books, affiliated with Paramount Productions, Gene Roddenberry, Fox Broadcasting or NBC Television. The History of Trek is a scholarly work intended to explore an American cultural phenemona and use TWIN PEAKS as a case study in the exploration of a cult television show.

Quotes attributed to specific periodicals are copyright by the respective publications cited.

First Printing 1991

GENE RODDENBERRY (1921—1991)

It came as a surprise to many when Gene Roddenberry died of a heart attack on October 24, 1991. While the news that he had suffered a series of strokes during the year had leaked out, the full extent of his illness had not.

There had been rumors, though, when a gala 25th anniversary celebration for STAR TREK at Paramount was scaled down in September when he was too ill to attend. But a couple of actors from the original series have long been rumored to be in frail health, but no one ever thought Roddenberry would be the first to depart.

While some fear that with Roddenberry's passing the light of STAR TREK will die, it has been known for some time that he was all but retired, having stepped down from his on-line duties on THE NEXT GENERATION more and more as each year passed until for the last two he has been little more than a consultant. His involvement with the motion pictures has been minimal since the first one, the only one he worked full time on.

STAR TREK was a synthesis of many talents. While it was created by Roddenberry over 25 years ago, it was developed by such people as Gene Coon, Dorothy Fontana and others whose contributions added much to the legend. While Roddenberry had the original vision and steered the ship on a true course, he was not the only one to dream the dream as his biggest gift was to inspire others to join his creation. The many forms of STAR TREK over the years serves as living testimonial.

When people die they face the danger of being elevated to a role they never had in life or ever aspired to. So one should not suddenly elevate Roddenberry to godhood after he no longer walks among us. Gene was a man with the foibles of a man but he should never be forgotten for his many abilities and most of all for his dream, a dream he shared with so many of us. This dream will insure that Gene Roddenberry will never be forgotten.

    —James Van Hise,
    November 11, 1991

A HISTORY OF TREK

INTRODUCTION:

A PHENOMENON UNEXCELLED

Star Trek. These two simple words bring a vast web of mental assoaciations to millions of people. The adventures of a remarkable group of characters have seemingly taken over a sizeable portion of our collective consciousness and made it their own. Perhaps the late science fiction visionary Philip K. Dick saw this when he had a character in his novel *A Scanner Darkly* refer to the latest entertainment extravaganza as a 'captainkirk'.

Now, as the twenty-fifth anniversary of the *Star Trek* phenomenon is underway, traces of the series are everywhere. In 1991's *Bill And Ted's Bogus Journey*, the teen heroes watch scenes from the first season *Star Trek* classic "Arena". The show gets more than an acknowledgement at the end of the credits; William Shatner is actually credited among the film's cast credits as portraying James Tiberius Kirk, a singular honor to be accorded to a sixty-second clip from an old television program.

But not just any old television program. This is a show that some people have dedicated a quarter century of their lives to, often making *Star Trek* a centerpiece of their own personal philosophies and mythologies. This is a show that refused to die. Battling network muddleheadedness in the sixties, creator Gene Roddenberry thought that his dream had died after its third season.

But nothing could undermine or destroy *Star Trek's* unique appeal. Rather than fade away gracefully into the dusty attic of quaint and anachronistic conceits, *Star Trek* stayed alive. Even Roddenberry was somewhat taken aback by the support his creation had gathered as the years went by; it was inevitable that *Star Trek* would return some day, despite the many impediments cast in its path along the way.

Star Trek brought fortune and fame to a handful of actors who had been laboring in obscurity for years.: Leonard Nimoy, William Shatner, DeForest Kelley, Nichelle Nichols, James Doohan, George Takei and Walter Koenig. Without them, this legacy may never have gotten off the ground. Instead, they became almost a surrogate family to a generation.

Even a disappointing *Star Trek: The Motion Picture* could not slow down this rampaging phenomenon. The death of Spock in *The Wrath of Khan* and the destruction of the Enterprise in *The Search for Spock* raised the ire and consternation of many fans, but it didn't keep them from seeing the films, and these traumas were passed through and became part of the legend themselves.

The Voyage Home brought the initial cycle to a rousing close, without any of the gut-wrenching changes of its two predecessors but still with plenty of action and human interest— and a few good laughs along the way. Not only that, the film series served to launch the directorial career of Leonard Nimoy, who went on to direct the smash hit *Three Men and a Baby*, starring Tom Selleck, Ted Danson and Steve Gutenberg.

Meanwhile, off on the horizon, another revolution was brewing: *Star Trek: The Next Generation*. Despite initial resistance and a disappointing first season, *The Next Generation* soon came into its own, becoming the most popular syndicated series in the history of television— and created a new roster of stars: Patrick

Stewart, Jonathan Frakes, Gates McFadden, Michael Dorn, Marina Sirtis and Brent Spiner as well as the gone-and-back-again Denise Crosby, who is presently the focus of a not-inconsiderable mystery.

Star Trek V: The Final Frontier, William Shatner's directorial debut, may have failed to achieve the monetary success of its predecessors, but the money-minded mavens at Paramount Pictures seem to realize that *Star Trek* is an inexhaustible gold mine. The end is not yet in sight.

Star Trek VI: The Undiscovered Country has already finished principal photography and is due for a Christmas 1991 release. Written and directed by Nicholas Meyer, it promises to bring Kirk and his crew's adventures to a satisfying conclusion, while providing links to *The Next Generation* as well.

Michael Dorn definitely has a role as a Klingon rumored to be Worf's grandfather. Spock's father Sarek has already appeared in the episode of *The Next Generation* bearing his name, in which it was revealed that Jean-Luc Picard was in attendance at Spock's wedding when he was a young lieutenant; this event is rumored to provide the concluding scenes of the latest big screen adventure. And in a final startling turn of events, Leonard Nimoy has signed to portray Spock in "Unification," a two-part episode of *The Next Generation* for broadcast in November 1991, and this should generate even more excitement over the imminent release of *The Undiscovered Country*.

All of this hullabaloo is not too bad for a concept that some thought would never make it off the ground, so to speak. All it took, however, was the creativity— and above all, the dedication and integrity— of the one man who put it all together: Gene Roddenberry.

—GUS MEYER

CHAPTER ONE:

A DREAM IN THE MAKING

Gene Roddenberry was a science fiction aficionado from childhood. It all started with a battered copy of *Astounding* magazine and took off from there. Still, he never considered writing in any genre or medium until much later in life.

In the late '40s he worked as an international airline pilot for Pan Am, and it was at this time that he began to write pieces for flying magazines. In 1948, he was one of only eight survivors of a plane crash in the Syrian desert, an experience that profoundly shaped his attitude toward life.

The writing bug soon led him to quit the airline and move to Los Angeles where he met with absolutely no success in the new field of television writing. The industry was, at the time, still centered on the east coast. This led him to become a Los Angeles policeman, a job which would provide him with insights no office job could ever hope to offer. At the same time, he continued to write, and sold his first script, pseudonymously, in 1951.

More sales followed, including "The Secret Defense of 117," a science fiction story which aired on *Chevron Theater* and starred Ricardo Montalban. During the same period, he wrote speeches for L.A. police chief William Parker, and even ghosted most of Parker's book *Parker On Police*, still regarded today as a classic of police philosophy.

Roddenberry managed to slip a bit of his own more liberal views into the right-wing Parker's texts; Parker was often perplexed when people he regarded as left-wingers would enthusiastically applaud his Roddenberry-penned speeches. Despite Parker's strong political stance, there was a side to him that impressed Roddenberry even more: he was always open to new ideas, and had wide-ranging intellectual interests, traits which Roddenberry would later incorporate into the character of Spock.

By 1954, Roddenberry's moonlighting was earning him four times his policeman's salary, leading him to resign from the force and devote all his energies to writing. After freelancing for a variety of series, in cluding *Dragnet, Naked City* and *Dr. Kildare*, he became head writer of the Richard Boone Western series, *Have Gun, Will Travel.*

He began to realize that freelancing left the final product of his mind in the hands of others. To retain control over his ideas (and to retain greater profits) he decided to become a producer. He had seen too many pilots written but left unmade; it was time for him to see one all the way through to completion.

His first series was thus created: *The Lieutenant,* which ran for the 1963 television season. Starring Gary Lockwood as a newly-commissioned officer in the peacetime Marine Corps, this was an intelligent, dramatic series which unfortunately failed to draw much of an audience. (Ironically, another Marine-centered series which premiered the following year was successful enough to last through the rest of the decade. *Gomer Pyle* was not, however, noted for its intelligence!) One episode featured an actor named Leonard Nimoy as a flamboyant Hollywood director; Roddenberry would eventually employ him again in the new series he was already creating.

By the time *The Lieutenant* went off the air, Roddenberry had already submitted a proposed *Star Trek* format to MGM, the studio behind The *Lieutenant* . The basic premise was the one now familiar to millions, but the characters were radically different.

The Captain was one Robert T. April, his executive officer was the logical female Number One, and the navigator was one José Tyler. The doctor character was nicknamed "Bones" but was otherwise an older, completely different character. Mr. Spock was in the proposal, but was described as having "a red-hued satanic look" and, according to one source, absorbed energy through a red plate in his navel!

The Enterprise and its mission are perhaps the only thing that made it to the screen unchanged from this original format. One other thing Roddenberry insisted on was that the science fiction in the show be ordered and logical, presenting the story with the same techniques that would be used in any other drama, without falling on convenient fantasy resolutions having no basis in reality.

MGM said they were interested, but not at the present time. Other studios followed suit, providing Roddenberry with a file full of politely worded brush-offs. A shift in the prevailing winds occurred when he learned that Desilu Studios was looking for series ideas. Desilu, the studio behind *I Love Lucy* and Lucille Ball's later shows, was hurting financially; *Lucy* was their only viable property, and they frequently rented out their facilities to other studios to make up for the monthly overhead costs. Desilu was impressed with Roddenberry and his ideas, including the *Star Trek* proposal, and signed him to a three-year pilot development deal. (Desilu's interest in *Star Trek* would pass over to Paramount Pictures when Paramount bought the television studio out.) Things seemed to pick up steam almost immediately, as Roddenberry was called in to pitch *Star Trek* to an assembly of CBS's highest ranking network executives.

They listened for two hours. Roddenberry was convinced that he'd sold them on it. They were certainly interested in his thoughts on saving costs and designing ships, among other things, but their questions turned out to have another motive entirely. When he was finished, they thanked him politely, but passed on the proposal, as they already had a science fiction series of their own in the works. Roddenberry may very well have inadvertently helped them launch *Lost In Space*, which even, by some coincidence, had the Robinson family embarking on a five-year mission of exploration. *Lost In Space* premiered in 1965, and, like *Star Trek*, ran for three seasons.

Roddenberry, even though disheartened by CBS' cavalier treatment of him, kept on trying. In May of 1964, NBC offered Roddenberry $20,000 in story development money. The deal was that Roddenberry would develop three story ideas for a *Star Trek* pilot, and then write a pilot script based on the idea chosen by the network. They chose the story entitled "The Cage." Roddenberry set to work on a shooting script. In September of 1964, the script was approved: the first *Star Trek* episode had received the green light.

Roddenberry had already been laying the groundwork for this. Of primary importance, was the starship Enterprise itself, which he hoped to have avoid all previous spaceship clichés.

The final design of the U.S.S. Enterprise was largely the work of assistant art director Matt Jeffries, who had a strong background in aviation.

During World War Two, Jeffries flew B-17 missions over Africa, and later devoted much of his spare time to restoring vintage airplanes. The starship and its various sets were drawn from Jeffries' own familiarity with aeronautics.

As a member of the Aviation Writer's association, Jeffries was able to collate a large number of designs from NASA and the defense industry...all as examples of what *not* to do. All previous science fiction spaceship designs were also held up as things to be avoided.

Hundreds of sketches were made for the design of the Enterprise; the main hull was, at one point, going to be spherical, and even the now-familiar final design almost wound up being shot upside down. Admittedly, this wouldn't make much difference in space. As a final touch of authenticity, red and green lights were added on the port and starboard sides, a time honored nautical practice. Finally, a three foot and fourteen-foot model of the Enterprise, were constructed.

Again, Matt Jeffries' Air Force engineering background came in handy in the design of the sets. The U.S. Navy was so impressed by the bridge design that they supposedly used it as a basis for one of their own communications centers.

Another seemingly insurmountable problem revolved around Roddenberry's desire to feature a green-skinned woman in the pilot. For some reason, all the make-up department's experiments failed to show up on the test footage shot of actress Susan Oliver for this purpose. No matter how dark they made the green, their model always showed up on film as looking perfectly normal. Eventually, they discovered that someone at the photo lab, perplexed by the pictures coming his way, was chemically correcting what he thought was a flaw in the initial photography. When this was cleared up, the desired make-up effect was achieved with a minimum of fuss.

"The Cage" began shooting with a cast of characters drawn from the original format, although the captain was now named Christopher Pike. Pike was portrayed by Jeffrey Hunter, who had the rare distinction of having once played Jesus Christ, in *King of Kings*. John Hoyt played the ship's doctor, Philip Boyce. Leonard Nimoy appeared as Spock, but the character was a bit different from its later developments, as the logical aspect of his future personality belonged to the character Number One, portrayed by Majel Barrett.

Leonard Nimoy had assumed that he would be trying out for the part of Spock; he failed to realize that he was Roddenberry's first and preferred choice for the role. The prospect of a regular series was exciting to the actor, who, despite his frequent guest appearances on television, did not have what could be called a stable income. He did have some misgivings about the part; what if the show was an unmitigated flop? Would he become a laughing stock, forever derided for having dared to don those silly-looking pointed ears? In conference with his friend Vic Morrow, he even pondered the possibility of developing character makeup that would completely conceal his true face— just in case *Star Trek* was a disaster and an embarrassment. Fortunately for his future recognizability, he thought better of this idea.

Still, one obstacle remained to be overcome. The makeup department had yet to come up with a painless means of applying the Spock ears. The ears were irritating and painful where the glue was applied; one of the reasons for Spock's general stiffness was the fact that any facial movement, however slight, served only to compound the intense physical discomfort generated by the aural appliances.

Matters were even more confounded by the odd fact that, due to contractual obligations, the actual ears had to be made by the props department, not the makeup department. Considerable variations in the shape of the ears (as well as in Spock's general appearance) can still be seen in the two pilot episodes. Leonard was frustrated by this situation, and expressed his dissatisfaction over it to his producer.

Roddenberry could tell that Nimoy's anguish was real— but what could he do? Finally, grasping at straws, he promised Nimoy that if, after thirteen episodes, he was still unhappy with the ears, Roddenberry would personally write an episode in which Spock had an ear-job to give him normal, human-looking ears. Nimoy pondered this, and then broke into laughter. The fate of the ears was sealed— and Spock still has them to this day.

"The Cage" introduces viewers to Roddenberry's nascent version of the Enterprise crew as it is headed towards a Starbase after a disastrous first contact with an alien culture. Captain Pike and his crew are tired and in great need of some rest, but they are distracted by a distress signal from a nearby planet.

When they investigate, they find a colony of scientists who have survived a crash, nearly twenty years earlier. . . and a beautiful young girl, Vina, who the survivors claim was born just as their ship crashed. Something seems odd, and when she lures Captain Pike away from the encampment, he is abducted by dome-skulled aliens and taken below the surface. The scientists and their camp, merely an illusion designed to lure humans, disappear.

Pike regains consciousness to find himself in an enclosed space; he has become part of an alien zoo, held prisoner by beings who can read his thoughts and project him into a bewildering variety of subjective but real-seeming scenarios. As he goes through these, he resists them at every turn, but begins to realize that the girl has a role in all this, too. Perhaps she is not an illusion, but another captive; she constantly tries to get him to accept his situation and make the best of the illusions his captors can provide.

Meanwhile, Number One and Spock haul out an impressive array of Federation technology in their attempts to free their Captain from his subterranean prison, but to no avail. Beneath the surface, the philosophical drama unfolds, with Pike finally being freed after resisting mind control. It is revealed that the woman, Vina, was the only survivor of the crash; not truly young, and disfigured by the crash, she elects to stay and live the rest of her life in the illusionary happiness the aliens will provide her. The aliens had been acting partly out of their own motivations but also out of a desire to help the lonely woman. Pike goes on to a Starbase while she embraces a reality that is false but which offers her the only comfort she will ever know.

NBC's reaction to this pilot was overwhelmingly enthusiastic. In its intelligence and its appearance, it surpassed anything done in the genre for television before, and looked better than the vast majority of theatrical science fiction films as well. No one had a bad word to say about the finished product.

They rejected it anyway.

The problem, it seemed, was that it was *too* intelligent. NBC was afraid that the story would go over the heads of most of the audience. Something a bit more action-oriented would perhaps be better, they mused, and, in an unprecedented move, gave Roddenberry a shot at a second pilot.

They also wanted to get rid of the guy with the pointed ears. There was always the possibility that religious groups might be offended by such a demonic looking character.

Roddenberry set out to revamp the entire show, but he was determined to keep Spock He discarded the character of Number One, who hadn't gone over too well, and promoted Spock to second-in-command, bringing him closer to the forefront.

This time, NBC wanted three complete scripts for consideration. All three had plenty of action: "Mudd's Women" by Stephen Kandel, "Omega Glory" by Roddenberry, and "Where No Man Has Gone Before" by Samuel A. Peeples. The network chose the Peeples script; the second *Star Trek* pilot was underway.

CHAPTER TWO:

A NEAR MISS
AND A SOLID HIT

Despite the network's misgivings, Roddenberry was determined to stick with Spock. He was also determined to maintain the Enterprise's multi-ethnic crew despite the network's concerns that this might affect ratings in various areas.

As for Spock, Roddenberry worked with the character a bit; the now-discarded Number One left a vacancy for the second-in-command, and Spock fit the bill perfectly. Spock also inherited Number One's cold, dispassionate logic. This all gelled to provide a fascinating amalgam of intelligence, restraint and a certain attractive aura of mystery, all admirably brought to life by a highly capable actor, Leonard Nimoy.

Leonard Nimoy was born in Boston in 1931, the son of Jewish immigrants from the U.S.S.R. He showed an early interest in the theater, making his stage debut in a production of "Hansel and Gretel" at the age of eight.

After high school, he studied briefly at Boston College. With only six hundred dollars to his name, he took a three day train trip to California in pursuit of an acting career. Studies at the Pasadena Playhouse did not lead to much movie work, however, and he was obliged to work at a variety of menial jobs: theater usher, ice cream counterman, pet shop clerk, vacuum cleaner salesman and many others.

A fluke break landed him the lead in a Z-grade boxing picture, *Kid Monk Baroni*, but this and a few much smaller roles in such forgettable pictures as *Frances Goes To West Point*, where he was billed far below the picture's talking donkey star, were all the film work he could obtain at the time.

After marriage and a stint in the Army in Georgia, Nimoy returned to Los Angeles in the late fifties and began to get more roles in episodic television, frequently as a heavy. He was far from being a household name.

In fact, although it was too early to realize it, it was his fortuitous encounter with Gene Roddenberry and *The Lieutenant* series that would save him from a career as one of those all-too-familiar faces whose name the audience can't quite place. *Star Trek* would soon preclude this possibility from ever coming true.

With Nimoy the sole holdover from "The Cage" pilot, Roddenberry was obliged to create an entirely new cast from scratch, and of course the most important character on any ship is the captain. Inspired by C.S. Forrester's heroic Horatio Hornblower character, Roddenberry created a new leader for the Enterprise, James Tiberius Kirk.

Kirk, a Midwesterner, is a driven officer with great faith in himself, who is not afraid to take a stand; apart from his senior officers, he confides in few, and bears the full responsibility for his command. Yet he is not without humor and he has a highly developed sense of adventure. For this all-important lead role, Roddenberry cast actor William Shatner.

William Shatner, thirty-eight at the time he started playing Captain Kirk, was born in Canada, where he attended McGill University and was, like Leonard Nimoy, involved in the theater quite early. By the time he graduated in 1952, Shatner had already done extensive radio acting work.

He then joined the National Repertory Theater of Ottowa, where he earned the massive sum of thirty-one dollars (Canadian) a week. After years of hard work he received excellent reviews in a New York production of Tamburlaine, but turned down a seven-year, five-hundred dollar a week (American) contract with Twentieth Century Fox in order to return to Canada and star in a television drama that he had written himself.

Soon afterward, he returned to New York and became extremely active in live television. He also played in the movie *The Brothers Karamozov*, which starred Yul Brynner. Work in Westerns soon followed. He settled in Los Angeles, determined to make his fortunes in Hollywood.

Roles on *Twilight Zone* and *Outer Limits* feature prominently in his resume from this period. He starred in the classic *Twilight Zone* episode "Nightmare At 20,000 Feet," and in the *Outer Limits* episode "Cold Hands, Warm Heart" he delivered, at one point, a passionate declaration about the importance of space exploration which sounds almost an exact paraphrase of the opening narration of every *Star Trek* episode.

For the technical end of things, Roddenberry came up with the character of the chief engineer, Montgomery Scott. A regular shirt-sleeves kind of guy, with an unbending devotion to his captain superseded only by his devotion to his ship. Scott would often be called upon to do the impossible, in as little time as he could manage. His ethnic background was suggested by the actor who played Scott. He was gifted in the area of dialects.and since there was a long tradition of Scotsmen in nautical and military engineering, his suggestion was approved.

Star Trek's other Canadian, James Doohan, was born in Vancouver, British Columbia, and flew an artillery observation plane in the Royal Canadian Air Force during the Second World War. Like many other actors of his generation, he did extensive radio work. He first came to the United States in 1946 and remained until 1953, acting and teaching acting.

In 1961 he came back to the United States and worked on such television shows as *Bonanza, Gunsmoke, Bewitched* and *The FBI*. Doohan had been offered the role of the chief engineer on *Voyage To The Bottom Of The Sea* right after he auditioned for *Star Trek* and only a call from the *Star Trek* offices at just the right time decided him on which series he would take. Of Scotty, Doohan once surmised that perhaps his accent was not natural, but was perhaps actually learned, possibly in a time when people would fall back and recreate archaic modes of speech in order to reduce the monotony of an ever more homogeneous language. An intriguing theory, indeed!

For the helmsman, who also doubles as weapons officer, Roddenberry created a character of Asian background, Sulu, who is primarily Japanese but also has Filipino blood. Sulu was portrayed by George Takei.

George Takei was born in Los Angeles but spent the World War Two period in Arkansas where, as a child, he lived with his family in a Japanese/American detention camp. He studied architecture at U.C. Berkeley and earned a Bachelor's degree at UCLA in 1960.

In the few years between this and the debut of *Star Trek*, he managed to appear on a number of shows, including *Perry Mason* and *I Spy*. He also acted in *From Hell to Eternity, The Green Berets,* and other movies.

He appeared in *The Twilight Zone* episode "The Encounter," an episode no longer included in the syndication package for reasons of anti-Japanese prejudice expressed in the script.

At a time when the networks were still dubious about the use of black characters in television (Bill Cosby's equal billing with Robert Culp on *I Spy* was definitely the exception, not the rule), Roddenberry pushed the envelope by creating the communications officer, Uhura.

Things were thrown more out of kilter when he made the character a woman as well. Even after the loss of the Number One character, he was determined to have a woman in a responsible position on the Enterprise bridge. In this, he was years ahead of our own military.

Uhura, whose name means freedom, was from an African nation (according to the background material, anyway), and is proof of the changes Earth society has achieved in Roddenberry's hopeful vision of the future.

Actress, dancer and singer Nichelle Nichols was cast as Uhura. Born in Chicago, she worked extensively as a vocalist, and toured with both Duke Ellington's band and with Lionel Hampton's. On stage, she appeared in such plays as *The Blacks, No Strings, Carmen Jones* and James Baldwin's *Blues For Mister Charlie*.

With the new cast set and ready to go, "Where No Man Has Gone Before" started shooting on July 21, 1965 and was not completed until January 1966, costing 330 thousand dollars to produce. Needless to say, the network was eager to see what they'd been waiting for.

Roddenberry and his team were on tenterhooks; would NBC reject this effort, too? In February, the word came through. *Star Trek* would debut in December, with the network committed to sixteen episodes. It was time to start producing the series. With a budget of roughly 180 thousand dollars an episode, it was going to be quite a ride.

Early on, the idea of incorporating the rejected "Cage" pilot into a two-part episode was put forward as a means of relieving the expected time-and-budget crunch. Set building, prop design, and, of course, scripts, all occupied a great deal of this preparation period.

Roddenberry attended the World Science Fiction Convention in Cleveland, Ohio on September 4, 1966, where he showed "Where No Man Has Gone Before" to a suitably impressed audience of five hundred die hard science fiction fans. Without Roddenberry, they would have had to settle for an episode of Irwin Allen's *Time Tunnel*.

"Where No Man Has Gone Before" was different from the form that *Star Trek* would soon assume. Uhura had not yet joined the roster, nor had Yeoman Janice Rand; the ship's doctor, Dr. Piper, was portrayed by Paul Fix; and Sulu was a physicist, not the helmsman. Several characters in key roles appeared only in the pilot.

What the Worldcon audience saw was the story of how the Enterprise tried to penetrate a mysterious purple energy barrier in space. Strange radiations affect the crew; Lieutenant Commander Gary Mitchell seems normal, but his eyes begin to glow silver. It soon becomes apparent that the radiation has boosted his latent extrasensory perceptions to a previously undreamed-of level. Mitchell's mental powers begin to accelerate, and Spock becomes convinced that Mitchell is a threat to the Enterprise and prompts Kirk to kill him.

But the Captain cannot bring himself to terminate an old friend from the Academy. Ultimately, Kirk and Mitchell battle to the death in a harsh landscape altered by Mitchell's godlike powers. At one point, Mitchell produces a tombstone bearing the name of James R. Kirk, proving that even a nearly omnipotent being can get someone's middle initial wrong. Finally, Kirk destroys Mitchell, but it is a hollow triumph, as he has killed the friend he once had.

The audience gave Roddenberry a standing ovation; he knew then that he was on the right track.

Finally, on September 8, 1966, *Star Trek* premiered on NBC. (Actually, the first broadcast was two days earlier, on Canadian television.) The episode aired was not the pilot (that was shown two weeks later) but the sixth episode filmed, "Man Trap," perhaps best known for its piteous Salt Vampire nemesis.

This episode was most notable in that it introduced audiences to a character who was not actually in the pilot, but who would quickly become an indispensable part of the *Star Trek* myths: Dr. Leonard "Bones" McCoy.

This seemingly cynical but strongly compassionate humanitarian would provide a constant counterpoint to the cold logic of Spock, and their battle of wits would soon become legendary.

Fed up with protocol, distrustful of technology (especially transporters) and wary of dehumanizing influences, in a way McCoy represents the probable reaction of an intelligent 20th century man cast forward into the 23rd century. He has his roots very much in our present. Veteran actor DeForest Kelley was the one called upon to bring this crucial character to life.

DeForest Kelley was born in Atlanta, Georgia, but bucked his Baptist minister father's desire for him to become a doctor and opted for acting instead. Moving to Long Beach, California, he continued the radio work he had begun in Georgia, and worked as an elevator operator.

In the Navy during World War Two, he worked in training films, where he was spotted by a talent scout from Paramount. He worked as a contract player at Paramount Studios for two and a half years. About this time, a fortune teller told him that he would not achieve success until after he passed the age of forty, which proved to be true!

Then, in 1948, he went to New York City and worked in television and on stage. Returning to Hollywood, he worked extensively in Westerns, both on television shows such as *Gunsmoke, Rawhide* and *Bonanza*, and in movies such as *Gunfight at the O.K. Corral* and *Warlock*. For Gene Roddenberry, Kelley starred in two pilots: 1960's *Free, Free, Free Montgomery*, in which he played a famous, controversial defense attorney named Jake Early, and in the unsold *Police Story* (no relation to the later TV series) as well.

With the key elements in place and the show finally in production and on the air, *Star Trek* was now more than a dream in Gene Roddenberry's mind. It was a reality. *Variety* insisted that the series wouldn't work; time has certainly proven them wrong.

CHAPTER THREE:

ONWARD
TO THE STARS WITH HOPE
(The First Season)

A week before *Star Trek* premiered, the *Buffalo Evening News* previewed the shows to come:

A 400-man space ship, the U.S.S. Enterprise, cruises the TV universe this fall starting Thursday night in Star Trek, NBC's expensive full-hour science fiction adventure series about puny man exploring the wide blue yonder. Starring the talented Canadian actor William Shatner as space ship commander Kirk, assisted by brainy, elf-eared Mr. Spock (Leonard Nimoy). Star Trek goes back and forth in time, jousting with alien spirits, bewildering viruses and ordinary human conflicts on a never-ending trip to other worlds.

NBC hopes the science fiction plots won't seem never-ending, and lays stress on the solid adventure approach.

"We're not going to be like the children's show, Lost In Space., where characters battle villains in eerie costumes," said star Shatner, coming back to earth on a lunch break. "We deal with human conflicts against a science fiction background." Using a Jekyll and Hyde plot in one episode, Captain Kirk becomes two men as he battles against his vicious animal self which is about to take over and destroy the great ship. Another show finds the space adventurers stricken by an insidious virus which eats away man's will. Poor Mr. Spock, who is half Vulcanian from the planet Vulcanis and thus trained to control his feelings, becomes a victim and undergoes a raging battle with himself, fighting emotional displays, which include crying scenes.

It should be noted that the odd variants on Mr. Spock's background in fact originated with the production company itself, and not from any journalist's error; the more familiar use of the name Vulcan to indicate both the planet and its people had not yet been quite solidified.

The Earth men have a few dandy tools and gadgets on display, all calculated to catch the fancy of young viewers. Captain Kirk and crew make excellent use of laser beam guns, jolting enemies with the sizzle of cutting light. They listen and understand various alien languages by way of walkie-talkie interpreters that translate foreign words in a split second.

"You know, a company is working on exactly the same gadget— a walkie-talkie interpreter," Shatner said. "That's the point of our show— science fiction projections into the future based on what is possible today."

Judged from Shatner's descriptions, Star Trek appears to be one step up from Lost In Space and Voyage to the Bottom of the Sea, in the way of adult entertainment. It's Twilight Zone, decked out in the razzle-dazzle of space uniforms, brilliantly lighted control boards, handsome hued space food and special effects gadgets— visual gimmicks, proven winners borrowed from Irwin Allen's adventure hits on modern man in the air and under water.

From these clumsy attempts to describe *Star Trek* 's technology, it is hard to guess that much of its terminology would actually be one day incorporated into common daily usage. The *News* writer went on to consider William Shatner:

. . . known for his Broadway roles and Shakespearean performances, [he] boldly goes all out in plugging his first Hollywood TV series.

"Star Trek," he asserts, "is going to be the best show on the air."

Two years ago, Canadian-born Shatner, a graduate of the Shakespearean theatre in Canada and England and with some fine cast credits from Broadway and serious TV drama, launched into a new series— For The People. He had high hopes. If you were among the smattering of viewers who watched, you may well recall the series dealt realistically with the personal and professional life of an assistant district attorney in New York City.

"I know now, but I didn't know then, the show was thrown away," Shatner said. CBS used For The People as a midwinter plugger against Bonanza. it faded with the first crocus next spring.

The new show would not suffer so slighting a fate. In fact, although Shatner could not tell at the time, it would make him world-famous. Again, on September 8, 1966, a new phase in his career was begun.

"The Man Trap," written by *Twilight Zone* alumnus George Clayton Johnson, kicked off the *Star Trek* series with a story featuring Dr. McCoy's apparent reunion with his old flame Nancy, now married to archaeologist Robert Crater. Unfortunately, Nancy is actually dead and is being impersonated by a creature that lives off the body salt of other living creatures.

This is further compounded by its ability to take on any form. McCoy is faced with the agonizing truth in a story that is quite poignant and moving. Oddly enough, the good doctor's futuristic medical supplies came out of the prop search for this episode, as futuristic salt shakers were sought out but then discarded for fear that they wouldn't be recognized as such. The props department, always on a budget, converted the saltshakers into medical devices.

The next episode aired, "Charlie X" featured Robert Walker, Jr. as a space foundling whose hidden psychic powers are ill matched with his adolescent need for attention and approval, in a story about loneliness and alienation. In hindsight, the story has more than passing similarities to the central character in Robert Heinlein's 1961 novel *Stranger In A Strange Land*.

"Where No Man Has Gone Before" was the third episode broadcast.

Things really hit their stride with "The Naked Time," which gave the *Star Trek* cast a chance to show off their range when an alien microbe opens up the ship's crew to their innermost personal conflicts. Kirk's love of the Enterprise wars with his knowledge that command keeps him from having a normal life.Spock's dual heritage leads to even more divided behavior, and he is seen to actually weep.

The ship, meanwhile, finds itself in danger of being destroyed, but is saved through the simple expedient of a little minor time-travel, the first time for the series. This episode also introduces Nurse Christine Chapel and her unrequited love for the unreachable Mr. Spock.

"The Enemy Within" gives Shatner a shot at strutting his stuff when a transporter malfunction divides him into two diametrically opposed selves. Believe it or not, this episode actually originated the much-abused concept of the "evil twin," and is perhaps the only time on TV that it was explored with any thought or imagination. Later, hack TV writers reduced the idea to a trivial cliche in the seventies and eighties on countless television shows.

"Mudd's Women," one of the three scripts proposed for the second pilot submission, introduces Roger C. Carmel as the rascally space swindler Harry Mudd. This also marks the first time the Enterprise is in dire need of fresh dilithium crystals. Furthermore, Mudd actually gives another character a pleasure drug, a fact overlooked by the network censor!

The October 15, 1966 *TV Guide* (two days after "Mudd's Women") featured a profile of William Shatner. Entitled "No One Ever Upsets The STAR,' it details Shatner's first taste of real fame.

William Shatner, Star Trek's 35-year-old Montreal-born ex-Hollywood holdout, sits in his plush Desilu dressing room force feeding himself on five pages of rush dialogue. He is interrupted first by a small man bearing a new-style jacket on a hanger, and then an intently solicitous press agent, and then an eager-to-please youth who asks in the manner of a bellhop addressing the man in the Presidential suite, "Would you like something cold to drink?"

Shatner orders, with thanks, a dietetic something and when the kid is gone closes his script and says in wonder, "Before, I always thought that kind of, uh, toadying was beneath human dignity. But for the first time I'm able to see the reason for it. These little attentions do help. It makes life easier for me."

A new Bill Shatner? Indeed?

. . .Shatner, who had a few years ago so assiduously shunned the Hollywood harness, was gleefully saying things like: "I've gotten great insight into the omnipotence of the series lead. Everybody does his best not to upset the star. It's an almost unique position few in the entertainment world achieve. . .it's like absolute power.' And he unleashes his machine-gun chuckle, his intelligent hazel eyes alight with huge appreciation of the ludicrousness of it all, at the same time thoroughly enjoying it.

He finishes his soft drink and moves to the rehearsal table outside his door, around which sit guest star Robert Walker Jr.; Nimoy, serious in his evil makeup and large, pointed ears; and director Larry Dobkin. Shatner has insisted on rehearsing here before moving to the set, an innovation most directors have applauded. As the

group begins the run-through, an associated producer arrives, clutching some late, late changes. Shatner mutters unhappily. "What's the matter," jibes the producer lightly. "You fighting to protect your lines?"

"I'm fighting for the ones I learned," Shatner says testily. Shatner would later take his beef to Roddenberry and be assured there would be no more last-second changes.

Roddenberry, a big, somewhat bashful man, admits that the thought of life with an assertive, stage-oriented actor did not send him into ecstasies of joyous anticipation and that the first day of shooting seemed to auger the worst. "He came in and said, 'I have a few comments about the script,' and I thought, oh no. . . "But it wasn't so bad. I have never had more intelligent suggestions and we used all of them," says the producer.

Another time, Shatner, an aspiring writer, came into Roddenberry's office with a story he had written. Recalls Roddenberry: "He wouldn't let me take it home to read. He insisted on reading it right there. So I fortified myself with a Scotch and prepared to suffer. But the story flowed and it was so damned poetic I caught myself wishing I could right that well. . ."

Did he buy the story? "No."

Shatner's writing ambition is just one of the escape hatches he keeps open. "I hang on to the thought that there's always Toronto. It's my security blanket." He pauses. "Not really. . . it's taken me half a lifetime to realize you can't go back." ``

"What Are Little Girls Made Of?" again features two Kirks (Shatner must have loved this!) when he is duplicated, in android form, by Nurse Chapel's fiancé Dr. Roger Korby. She's been searching for him, but he seems to have gone just a little bit 'round the bend, and is intent on taking over the Enterprise and populating the universe with his androids, one of whom, Ruk, is portrayed by Ted Cassidy (Lurch on *The Addams Family*). This episode has a strange, eerie quality about it, and writer Robert Bloch peppers it with arcane references to aspects of H.P. Lovecraft's mythos. Kirk's brother George is mentioned in this episode.

"Miri" brings Kirk and crew to a planet remarkably like Earth, where ancient children live long lives until their long-delayed puberty causes them to sicken and die. Kirk is beaten up by children in this episode; McCoy finds a cure for the aging disease before almost succumbing to it himself.

"Dagger Of The Mind" involves Kirk's discovery of the abuses of power at a supposedly humane penal colony. This introduces the Vulcan mind meld, which conveniently served as a means to avoid a lengthy expository conversation with a mentally deranged character.

"The Corbomite Maneuver" was actually the third episode filmed, as well as being the first one to include McCoy as a character. Here, Kirk encounters a massive, threatening space ship that is not what it seems to be.

The next two broadcasts consisted of a two-parter, "The Menagerie," which incorporated much of the footage from the first pilot, "The Cage." Here, Spock goes to great lengths to take Captain Pike, crippled in an accident, back to Talos IV so that he can live out his life in a happy illusion created by the Talosians. Through flashbacks, Spock explains his actions to Kirk and the others.

By this point in the series, one thing was crystal clear: Mr. Spock, originally a supporting character, was becoming as popular as the lead, Captain Kirk. At times, Shatner even felt obliged to remind some series scriptwriters that *he* was the Captain; he later acknowledged that there was sometimes friction between him and Leonard, but made certain to indicate that this was a matter of the past: "We went through that fire together and today we are fast friends. Leonard is an honest man and a fine craftsman." Still, at the time Shatner was so concerned over the situation that he counted his lines in each new script to be certain that he had more than Nimoy. If he didn't, either more were added for him at his insistence, or Nimoy's lines were cut.

Norman Spinrad once related the story of his visit to the set of the episode he had scripted, "The Doomsday Machine," and witnessed the director trying to come up with an alternative way for Nimoy to react to Shatner in a scene because for Nimoy to utter a line would have given him one line too many as far as Shatner was concerned.

But by the end of 1966, *Star Trek* was already in trouble. NBC was dissatisfied with the Nielsen ratings, and were, as usual, uncertain of how to categorize the series. The show had already generated a highly positive response in the science fiction subculture, of course, and so Roddenberry turned to Harlan Ellison for help. Perhaps if the network knew just how large an audience science fiction fandom represented, they might very well see the show in a new light.

And so, Ellison sent out five thousand letters urging science fiction fans to press NBC with a letter-writing campaign. Dated December 1, 1966, Ellison's missive bore the letterhead of "The Committee," an impressive listing of names: Paul Anderson, Robert Bloch, Lester Del Rey, Ellison, Philip José Farmer, Frank Herbert, Richard Matheson, Theodore Sturgeon and A.E. Van Vogt. Thus, Ellison, who would later be less than keen on his involvement with *Star Trek* ("The City on the Edge of Forever" had yet to be filmed), was in fact responsible for the very first letter campaign raised to benefit the series.

This, of course, was in the days when the Nielsen ratings presupposed a bland, all-encompassing uniformity belonging to the "average" TV viewer. With this sort of *a priori* approach, it is hardly surprising that the appeal of *Star Trek* did not dovetail with the Nielsen company's concepts, and hence eluded their comprehension. But in those pre-demographics days, before the variety of the American mindset was taken into consideration, the Nielsen ratings were the voice of God as far as the networks were concerned. Those were the numbers that determined a show's advertising value and marketability, as well as its popularity, whatever evidence reality had to offer to the contrary.

And evidence there was. The stars of *Star Trek* had become wildly popular with the public. . . almost, if not quite, overnight. The ratings problem seems almost ironic when held up against this fact.

In 1966, Leonard Nimoy and William Shatner were invited to appear in Hollywood's annual Christmas parade. This newfound fame was no guarantee of respect, however, for while the parade announcer got Shatner's name correct, he introduced the other *Star Trek* star as "Leonard Nimsy." Despite this gaffe, Nimoy was, for the first time in his life, frequently recognized on the street, and constantly besieged for autographs.

He took it all in good humor, although he soon became weary of smart-aleck fans asking him where he'd left his ears. Fan mail began to pour in, too, a great deal of it from younger viewers.

All of this was uncharted territory for Nimoy. At first, he was determined to answer all his fan mail by himself. Thirty or so letters a week was no big deal, after all. Unfortunately for this plan, the numbers began to increase every week, until thousands of messages were pouring in. He had to hire an assistant, Teresa Victor, to help him cope with his popularity; the other *Star Trek* stars made similar arrangements.

With the success of the show, the principal actors were better off financially than they had been in their entire careers. Nimoy used this to upgrade his personal transportation, and replaced his battered old car with a new Buick luxury car. Shatner went for something sportier, while DeForest Kelley bought a Thunderbird— which he managed to ram into Nimoy's Buick one day at the end of shooting. Things proceeded amicably, but passers-by were probably a bit nonplussed to see a normal looking man exchanging insurance information with Leonard, who was still rigged up in full Spock regalia.

There was also a down side to Nimoy's newfound celebrity. Early in *Star Trek*'s run, NBC arranged for him to be the Grand Marshall of Medford, Oregon's annual Pear Blossom Festival; this was to be his first real promotional trip, and he was quite unprepared for the chaos that would surround it. The parade went without a hitch—but it had also been announced that Nimoy would sign autographs in a small park at the end of the parade route. A crowd, with a large number of young people, actually followed Leonard's itinerary. By the time he reached the park, it was swarming with immense numbers of people. The lone park employee was swamped by this madness; traffic was completely fouled up. In the end, Medford police had to make their way in and "rescue" Nimoy from the friendly mob.

Eventually, it reached the point where people ac-

tually turned down the chance for a Spock/Nimoy appearance. Macy's, the famous New York department store, declined to have Nimoy appear to promote one of his record albums. They honestly admitted that they could not handle the sort of crowds which would undoubtedly attend such an event.

Nimoy himself turned down many requests for public appearances because they asked for him to wear the ears in public; he estimated losing about fifty thousand dollars by passing up these offers.

His popularity continued to manifest itself in a bewildering variety of ways. Spock was the only *Star Trek* character to merit solo reproduction as a model kit. While Kirk and Sulu did join Spock as small figures in AMT's Enterprise Bridge model, a six-inch tall Spock was featured in a larger diorama kit which featured him facing off against a three headed alien serpent. (In 1975, Spock and other *Star Trek* characters would have the dubious honor of being reproduced as popsicle molds!)

His face also appeared on a variety of series-related toy packages over the years, including 'sixties-vintage phaser rifles and the ever-popular *Star Trek* disc gun. "I Grok Spock" buttons, referring to Robert A. Heinlein's classic 1961 science fiction novel *Stranger In A Strange Land,* began to crop up as well.

By this point, the NBC executives who had wanted to give Spock the axe were now acting as if they'd been for the character all along. Leonard's place in the public consciousness was rock solid, and the first season wasn't even over yet!

"The Conscience of the King" involves Kirk in efforts to determine whether an actor is actually the man responsible for a massacre some years earlier; Kirk is one of the few survivors. An intriguing study of guilt and self punishment, with an intriguing plot twist or two, it is ably supported by actor Arnold Moss in a very demanding role.

"Balance of Terror" introduces the Romulans, who have returned after a century to harass the Federation with the assistance of their new cloaking devices. This story, essentially a submarine movie set in space, featured Mark Lenard as the Romulan commander. Lenard would, of course, play Spock's father Sarek in a future episode.

"Shore Leave," written by Theodore Sturgeon, prefigures the movie *Westworld* by some years, as the crew beams down for R & R on a planet that seems to be deadly but is actually an artifact programmed to custom tailor amusements for each individual. This marks the first time a leading *Star Trek* character dies, only to return intact. (This time around it's McCoy.)

"The Galileo Seven" brings Spock to the forefront as he commands a shuttlecraft which crashes, leaving him, Scotty and Dr. McCoy stranded on a hostile planet. Is his logic sufficient to save the castaways, or must he learn to look at things from an irrational perspective?

"Squire of Gothos" is Trelane, who traps the Enterprise and her crew to be his playthings; he is a powerful godlike being, but also a child, ultimately answerable to its parents. . . but not before shaking up the resolute Captain Kirk a bit.

"Arena" adapts the classic science fiction story by Fredric L. Brown and casts Kirk in the lead, as the Captain and the lizard-like Gorn are chosen as champions of their respective races by the meddlesome superior Metrons.

"Tomorrow Is Yesterday" is the first solid time-travel story for *Star Trek,* in which the Enterprise is hurled back to the 20th Century by the gravitational field of a black hole. Matters are complicated when an Air Force jet spots the Enterprise and Kirk must decide what to do with pilot John Christopher.

In "Court-Martial" Captain Kirk is tried for criminal negligence which resulted in the death of an officer; the redoubtable Mr. Spock applies his logic to the case and ultimately proves that the officer is really alive, having staged his own death in order to satisfy a personal grudge against Kirk.

Sulu gets to go nuts onscreen in"The Return of the Archons," in which the Enterprise investigates the planet Beta III, which is ruled by mysterious computer. (The last Federation ship to visit, a century earlier, was called the Archon, hence the returning archons of the title are Kirk and his crew.) The outsiders are threatened with absorption, but Kirk ultimately talks the ancient computer into destroying itself. Spock actually hits someone in this episode.

"Space Seed" introduces Ricardo Montalban as Khan, a late-twentieth-century fanatic who, with his followers, has been adrift in a "sleeper ship' for hundreds of years. The Enterprise revives the sleepers only to be taken over by Khan, who uses the infatuation of Marla McGivers, a young woman officer, with him in order to gain control by cutting off the air to the bridge. At the end he is defeated (Kirk retaliates with knockout gas in the ventilation system) and chooses exile on an unexplored planet for himself and his people. McGivers chooses to join him.

"A Taste of Armageddon" draws Kirk into a peculiar war between the planets Eminiar Seven And Anan Seven: battles are no longer fought, but computers do the fighting and determine the casualties. Victims in the affected areas then willingly report for euthanasia. Kirk is appalled by this, of course, and all the more so when the Enterprise is decreed a casualty of war.

Kirk and crew destroy the computers and leave the two worlds faced with the options of real war on one hand and peaceful negotiations on the other.

"This Side of Paradise" takes the Enterprise to a colony that should have died of radiation poisoning years earlier, but survived because of spores on the planet Omicron Ceti III that also provide a constant sense of euphoria. The crew all fall prey to this, rendering them all unfit for (and uninterested in) their duties. Foremost among these is Spock, who once again has his emotions liberated as in "The Naked Time." He falls in love with a young botanist who he had known before. Kirk must discover a way to get his crew back; Spock's happy romance is unfortunately short lived. (He is also referred to as a Vulcanian on the show for the first and last time, since the terminology still hadn't been standardizes!)

About this time, *TV Guide* featured a profile of Leonard Nimoy (March 4,1967).

It could only happen in America: where else could a son of Russian immigrants become a television star with pointed ears?

The article then describes the picture of "The Spock Cut" in Max Nimoy's Boston barber shop, which he would proudly point out as his son to all customers; Nimoy's mother Dora was sometimes interrupted at her job in a department store by people wanting to look at Spock's mother. The article went on:

Leonard Nimoy, who gets much of his fan mail from younger viewers, says, "The kids dig the fact that Spock is so cool." Star Trek's creator-producer, Gene Roddenberry, has a more profound explanation of the character's appeal: "We're all imprisoned within ourselves. We're all aliens on this strange planet. so people find identification with Spock." But actress Evelyn Ward, who went to drama school with Nimoy when both were new to Hollywood, attributes the attraction of Spock to the "great animal magnetism" of Leonard Nimoy himself.

For years this magnetism was pretty well hidden on TV and in movies by a succession of Indian and Mexican makeups. But when Gene Roddenberry, who was then producing The Lieutenant, cast Nimoy in an episode of that series a few seasons ago, he said to himself, "If I ever do a science fiction show, I'm going to put pointed ears on him and use him."

Like most serious actors in the comic-strip world of series television, Leonard Nimoy attempts to give the character he plays more depth than a pair of pointed ears and slanted eyebrows might indicate: "I don't want to play a creature or a computer. Spock gives me a chance to say something about the human race." On a more practical level, he add, "A television series can either be a beginning or an end. I have all sorts of things I want to do. Perhaps this show will give me the wherewithal to do some of them." But on the most practical level of all, he admits, "I'm having a ball. It's the first steady job I've had in seventeen years."

Except for the Spock haircut, which he does not alter off screen, Nimoy does not look like an actor. He is a quiet, serious man with shell-rimmed glasses, which not only correct his farsightedness but also hide the half-shaved eyebrows that are extended upward during the hour and a half of makeup which produces Mr. Spock. Only his parents and a few old friends call him "Lenny." On the set, where nicknames are almost de rigueur, he is always addressed as Leonard, which may be a tribute to the dignity he brings to the character he plays. His makeup man, Fred Phil-lips,swears that he can see Nimoy's personality become that of Spock as he puts on the makeup. "It begins to take place as the eyebrows go on—after the ears."

"The Devil In The Dark" is the Horta, a silicon based creature that has been killing miners in the underground colony of Janus IV. The Enterprise is called in on the crisis, but Spock discovers, by means of the Vulcan mind meld, that it is actually a mother protecting its young, in this case spherical eggs which had previously seemed only peculiar geological phenomena. The real conflict of this story is the need to overcome the fear and hostility of the human miners when they are faced with something new and incomprehensible.

The Horta costume, designed and worn by Janos Prohaska, was originally used in the last *Outer Limits* episode, "The Probe," but was customized and refurbished for its appearance on *Star Trek*.

"Errand of Mercy" sends Kirk to the peaceful pastoral world of Organia, which is in danger of Klingon attack; Klingon/Federation relations have become increasingly strained, and war seems imminent. When Commander Kor and his Klingon force invade and take over, they arrest Spock and Kirk, but the Organians themselves seem unperturbed by the occupation. The Organians do rescue Kirk and Spock, and avert war by the use of their previously unsuspected mental powers, which render all weapons ineffective.

They are in fact completely evolved beings whose human forms were a disguise, and they promise to keep a watchful eye on the enemy factions. In spite of the major element represented by the Organians and their ability to force an end to war, they were never used again in any subsequent *Star Trek* episode

"The Alternative Factor" involves the battle between Lazarus and his anti-matter double Lazarus; the fate of the universe hangs in the balance, and once again hinges on the need for dilithium crystals.

"The City on the Edge of Forever" is generally regarded as one of the best *Star Trek* episodes; it is also perhaps the episode with the most interesting background history. Harlan Ellison's original script was rewritten by Gene Roddenberry, perhaps unnecessarily, and has become a longstanding source of annoyance for the writer. Roddenberry's reasons have become somewhat clouded with the passage of time; he has claimed that Ellison's script included huge crowd scenes and other factors which would have drastically exceeded the show's budget (not exactly true) and even that the script had Scotty dealing drugs!

Ellison's original draft did hinge on a low ranking crew member dealing in illegal drugs, but it was not Scotty by any means; perhaps Roddenberry was simply aghast that someone might dare to show a seamy underside to his perfect human civilization of the future. The script as written by Ellison was published in the now-out-of-print *Six Science Fiction Plays*, edited by Roger Ellwood, and is due to be published again soon. . . with an extensive introduction by Ellison detailing the controversy in all its gory details. But, despite Ellison's disavowals of the filmed product, his original story still shines through Roddenberry's rewrite, and the story retains its fascination.

In the story as filmed, Dr. McCoy accidentally injects himself with a powerful, experimental drug and becomes completely unhinged. (Apparently Roddenberry would rather impugn the good doctor's basic competency rather than allow the blame to rest with a dishonest drug-smuggling crewman.) Meanwhile, Kirk and Spock are investigating a mysterious time portal, the Guardian of Forever, on the planet below.

McCoy beams down and leaps through the portal, disappearing into the past; the Enterprise suddenly ceases to exist, leaving Kirk and Spock stranded in a distant corner of the universe. They must go to the past and undo whatever it is McCoy has done to disrupt history; in 1930s New York, Kirk falls in love with Edith Keeler (Joan Collins), not realizing that she is the key to their predicament.

Spock manages to create a time scanning device with his tricorder and the primitive technology of the period, and ultimately discovers that Keeler will, if she lives, lead a pacifist movement that will keep the USA out of World War Two. The Nazis will win the war and make history on Earth a veritable hell; Keeler's humanitarian impulses contain the seeds of humanity's destruction.

Kirk must then force himself to keep the still delirious McCoy from saving Edith from her death under the wheels of a car. History is restored to its proper form, but not without some wrenching decisions for Kirk.

This was to be DeForest Kelley's favorite episode of the series. According to him, the catalytic character was originally a guest star but was altered to accommodate McCoy.

"Operation: Annihilate" features William Shatner in a second role: that of the dead body of Kirk's older brother George, complete with a mustache and gray hair. This personal tragedy is discovered on the planet Deneva, where alien parasites are attacking humans and driving them to their deaths with excruciating pain. This episode's effectiveness is somewhat underscored by the fact that the creatures look like enormous airborne fried eggs. Held to a wall with electromagnets, these creatures fell to the ground quite convincingly when hit by phaser fire.

This episode brought the first season to its end. Leonard Nimoy would be nominated for Best Supporting Actor in a Dramatic Series for this year's work.

Between seasons, Nichelle Nichols was profiled in TV Guide (July 15, 1967):

"The producers admit being very foolish and very lax in the way they've used me—or not used me."

Producer Gene Coon demurs: "I thought it would be very ungallant to imperil a beautiful girl with twenty-toed snaggle-toothed monsters from outer space." But executive producer Gene Roddenberry is coming around: "We're thinking about taking her down on the planets next season. Maybe we'll have wardrobe make her an appropriate costume for planet wear."

The canny Miss Nichols has already finagled an increase in her dialogue quotient as communications officer. Her lines have run to such emotionless phrases as "All hailing frequencies open, sir," or "This frequency is open, sir." Once in exasperation she blurted out: "Mr. Spock, if I have to say "Hailing frequencies open' one more time, I'll blow my top! Why don't you tell me I'm a lovely young woman?" Her ad-lib improvisation was instantly incorporated in the script.

This last assertion, unfortunately, is not borne out by a careful examination of the seventy-nine known episodes of *Star Trek*.

Actually, Nichelle Nichols was so dismayed by her character's limitations that she considered quitting the show after the first year. But when she met civil rights leader Martin Luther King, Jr., he told her to stay with it; just by being on the show, a bridge officer in a position of responsibility, she was providing a positive message that would be beneficial both to blacks and to the perception of blacks by others. (And somewhere in Brooklyn, the girl who would someday take the stage name of Whoopi Goldberg *was* inspired by Lieutenant Uhura.)

Of the famous tension between Spock and McCoy, DeForest Kelley tried to use elements of comedy and drama in the relationship, in a 1974 interview with Joseph Gulick:

I just gently tried to mix it with McCoy because of the unique situation that was involved between Spock and McCoy. I never wanted it thought for a minute that McCoy truly disliked him, because he didn't. McCoy had great respect for Spock and I thought and felt that the best way, was to somehow lighten it with an expression or a line. I did that very purposefully. I didn't want to lose fans by being too hard with Spock under certain circumstances. McCoy liked him. It became a kind of battle of wits.

Leonard [Nimoy] and I both worked on these things, you know. We discussed them at great length, as to how they should be played. we all felt very deeply about the show and worked very hard on it. The show is unique inasmuch as that between scenes we never sat down and read a book. Usually on a motion picture set you'll see an actor reading the trade papers or something between scenes. Not on Star Trek. The whole cast always went to the rehearsal table with the director and we began to break down future scenes that we were going to do and work at a table between scenes, very much like they used to do between scenes of live television in New York. This had a great bearing on the show. No one was out just running around or loafing or sleeping in a dressing room. They were preparing for the next scene.

We generally shot seven days, depending on the script, depending on the script. We even went eight days on them. We worked long hours, and there were many nights until eight-thirty or nine.

Leonard and I both had early make-up calls. We had a very large cast, so our make-up calls were around six or six-thirty in the morning. On many nights we would not get home until ten. You just have something very light to eat and go to bed, and you're up again the next morning at five.

That was our first year. The second year they began to be a little more organized and they were able to schedule things so it really wasn't so rough on us. The first year was pure hell, but I think we did our best work in the first year when I look back.

CHAPTER FOUR:

STEADY AS SHE GOES
(The Second Season)

During the spring and summer of 1967, while the first season of *Star Trek* was in reruns, word began to spread that the next season would feature a visit to Spock's home planet, Vulcan. Needless to say, speculation was rife. That year in New York, World Science Fiction Convention attendees were the first to see the promised episode, "Amok Time," as well as the first season's blooper reel.

"Amok Time," written by veteran science fiction writer Theodore Sturgeon (who also wrote the first season's "Shore Leave") proved to be well worth the wait. Keying in on the interest in Spock's emotional chinks, the story opened with the Vulcan officer acting decidedly strange and sulky.

McCoy determines that Spock will die if something is not done about the physical changes he's undergoing, and Spock admits, not to the doctor but to Kirk, that he is undergoing *pon farr*, the Vulcan mating cycle, which will, indeed, be fatal if he doesn't get to Vulcan and undergo the proper rituals posthaste. Kirk bucks orders and reroutes the Enterprise to Vulcan.

The rituals involved are remnants of Vulcan's barbaric past (one wonders if they're really prudes except on these occasions). T'Pau, a dignified Vulcan leader, appears, as does the first use of the Vulcan ritual greeting "Live long and prosper." (Leonard Nimoy provided the accompanying hand gesture, which he 'borrowed' from an important Jewish religious ritual; congregations were supposed to look away when the rabbi made this gesture, but Nimoy, as a young boy, couldn't help but peek!) Spock's would-be bride (by long-standing pre-arrangement, of course) T'Pring ads danger to the proceedings when she demands that Spock must engage in combat for her hand, and she chooses Kirk as her champion. The fight must be to the death. Fortunately, McCoy manages to set up Kirk's "death" in order to end the fight. Spock snaps out of *pon farr* thanks to this ruse, and is greatly relieved to find Kirk still alive; T'Pau gets Kirk out of any potential hot water by asking the Federation to divert the Enterprise to Vulcan.

Vulcan was presented here in sparse but effective visual terms; T'Pau, as portrayed by Peter Lorre's one-time wife Celia Lovsky, carries the entire implied culture in her bearing. Sturgeon provided many small but telling touches regarding ethics and custom of the planet Vulcan; photography and music added immensely to this episode. The Worldcon audience was suitably impressed.

The cast of *Star Trek* was altered to include a new character in the second season, as well. The network was pressing for a character to rope in the "youth" market, something along the lines of Davey Jones of *The Monkees*. A press release (later revealed to have exaggerated the truth by fabricating the incident) claimed that the show was criticized by the Russian Communist newspaper *Pravda* for, among other things, its lack of a Russian character in the Enterprise's otherwise multinational crew. And so to kill two birds with one stone, Roddenberry supposedly created the character of Ensign Pavel Chekov, a young officer with a heavy accent, to satisfy Soviet angst. Signing on as Chekov was actor Walter Koenig.

The second season of *Star Trek* began on September 15, 1967. The episode shown was "Amok Time," which also marked the first time DeForest Kelley received billing in the opening credits of the show.

"Who Mourns for Adonis?" brings the Enterprise into conflict with no less a personage than the Greek god Apollo, actually the last of a band of immortals who once visited Earth and lived on Mount Olympus. Scotty has a romantic interest here, but she falls for the god instead. Fortunately, Kirk manages to obtain her aid in destroying the temple that provides the god with his omnipotent powers, and Apollo destroys his own physical form and lets the Enterprise go. (In James Blish's adaptation of this episode, a final epilogue note from the original script is retained: the young woman is found to have become pregnant by the god Apollo.)

"The Changeling" is Nomad, an ancient Earth probe which has merged with an alien device and is convinced that its mission is to destroy imperfect life forms. Unfortunately, humans fit its criteria perfectly. Fortunately, it thinks Kirk is the scientist Roykirk, the scientist who created it. Thus, it repairs Scotty after killing him out of deference to Kirk. It is still a threat, but Kirk manages to trick it into destroying itself. (In retrospect, this seems to have been one of his specialties.)

"Mirror, Mirror" casts Kirk, McCoy, Scotty and Uhura into an alternative universe where the Federation developed along bloodthirsty, Klingonesque lines. Meanwhile, their mirror counterparts arrive on the regular Enterprise, where Spock has the sense to toss them all in the brig. In the alternate universe, Kirk and crew meet, among others, a brutal and scarred Sulu, an ambitious Chekov, a 'Captain's Woman' (!) and a bearded Spock. Kirk uses logic to win Spock2's assistance in his efforts to return home.

"Mirror, Mirror," written by Jerome Bixby, was awarded the Hugo Award by science fiction fandom.

"The Apple" is the gift Kirk brings to the peaceful, Eloi-like inhabitants of a dangerous world where their existence is protected by an ancient computer which also has retarded their social development. The Prime Directive notwithstanding, Kirk completely destroys their social order and saves the Enterprise as well.

"The Doomsday Machine" was shot from a script by Norman Spinrad and featured William Windom as Commodore Matthew Decker, the sole survivor of the crew of the U.S.S. Constitution (an AMT model kit, apparently 'damaged' with a Zippo lighter). His crew was on a planet destroyed by the device of the title, which seems to be a planet-destroying weapon apparently built by a long-dead civilization. Decker is obsessed with destroying it, a latter-day Captain Ahab in space, and hijacks the Enterprise to this end.

When Kirk regains control, Decker steals a shuttlecraft and dies trying to destroy the weapon. Kirk himself then flies the Constellation into the device's maw and sets it to self-destruct, transporting out in barely the nick of time, destroying the device for good.

"Catspaw" was aired, appropriately enough, just before Halloween 1967 (on October 27, to be exact). Written by Robert Bloch, it involves the efforts of two shape changing aliens to frighten the Enterprise crew with all the accoutrements of human superstition: magic, skeletons, witches and the like. At one point, Kirk, Spock and McCoy are chained in a dungeon; Kirk turns to address the doctor as "Bones," only to find a skeleton dangling in his friend's place. This macabre humor is further perpetuated by Spock's inability (fortunate in these circumstances) to comprehend any of the illusions thrown his way as frightening in any way, shape or form. A final touch of pathos is introduced at the end when the aliens assume their true shapes and are found to be feeble, helpless creatures.

"I, Mudd" brings back Roger C. Carmel as Harry Mudd, currently serving as Emperor of a planet of advanced androids. Of course, the androids realize what a buffoon he is but are using him to further their own plans of universal domination, which they plan to begin by stealing the Enterprise. Kirk and crew, including Spock, bewilder the androids by acting in absurd ways, and Mudd, who has created himself a beautiful android harem, is punished by being afflicted with innumerable android replicas of the nagging, shrewish wife he'd abandoned long before.

"Metamorphosis" introduces Zephram Cochrane, the inventor of the warp drive. . . who was believed to have died a century before at the age of eighty seven. It seems that he met a nebulous space creature who has kept him alive ever since; it has diverted the Galileo shuttlecraft to his location in order to provide him with human companionship. Cochrane begins to fall in love with the terminally ill Nancy Hedford, a Federation functionary, who was being taken to the Enterprise. Kirk uses a translator to communicate with the alien companion and discovers that it is in love with Cochrane. Cochrane is initially repulsed by this, but accepts it when the immortal being merges with the dying woman, who stays with the scientist as the Enterprise resumes its course.

"Journey to Babel" finally introduces Spock's parents, the Vulcan Sarek (Mark Lenard) and his human wife Amanda (Jane Wyatt). The occasion is a diplomatic mission. A ship is following the Enterprise; the Tellerite ambassador is murdered and Sarek is the prime suspect. Sarek needs a blood transfusion for a heart operation but Spock must act as captain after an Andorian stabs Kirk. Kirk fakes his recovery so Spock can give blood. A battle with the ship results in its destruction. Kirk's attacker kills himself after revealing that he killed the Tellerite ambassador, and Spock and his father achieve a rapprochement after nearly twenty years of estrangement.

In December 1967, another letter campaign came to the rescue of the again-beleaguered series. This one, orchestrated by fan Bjo Trimble and her husband John, was even more successful than the first. Inspired by NBC's decision to cancel the show, it generated an unprecedented number of letters, and would prove instrumental in leading to the show's third season.

New Year's Day, 1968, saw the *Star Trek* season's continuation with a perhaps unintentional Christmas touch: an episode wherein a child is born in a cave. "Friday's Child" opens with a briefing on how to get along in Capellan society.

Kirk and crew are headed for Capella IV to head off a potential alliance between that world and the Klingons, but the good captain doesn't seem to have learned much about the required protocol. The planet's leader is deposed and his wife seems fated to die, but Kirk interferes and the Klingons turn the Capellans against him and his team. McCoy helps the woman deliver her baby, who is ultimately named the new ruler when the Klingons kill the latest ruler; the child is named 'Leonard James' after McCoy and Kirk, but Spock, not much for children it seems, gets short shrift.

"The Deadly Years" afflicts Kirk and his main officers with a deadly disease causing accelerated aging. Spock ages the slowest thanks to the longevity of Vulcan's, but McCoy's efforts to find a cure are hampered by his own senescence. A Commodore on board convenes a hearing and removes the now nearly-senile Kirk from command. He then takes the Enterprise right into the Neutral Zone, where a serious run-in with Romulans is averted through means of the old reliable Corbomite maneuver, executed by a Kirk restored to normalcy by McCoy's timely discovery of a remedy for the aging disease.

This rated as another of DeForest Kelley's favorite episodes. Again speaking to Joe Gulick in 1974, he observed: "I enjoyed doing ["The Deadly Years"] because it gave me an opportunity to do something that I would never be called upon to do." As his character aged, Kelley had him become more and more the old-fashioned country doctor McCoy really envisioned himself as. "Yes, I began to fall back. I had that in mind from the beginning, that the older he became, the more he would fall back into what he really had a feeling in his heart for. Fortunately, it worked very well. There was a great disturbance at the studio at the time because they felt I should have been nominated for that show, but I was not. They were very upset about it." Nimoy, however, would again receive an Emmy nomination for the second season.

In "Obsession" the Enterprise is attacked by a gaseous being that lives off of human blood. Fortunately, the first crewman it attacks is Spock, and it flees, presumably with an unpleasant, copperlike taste in its "mouth." Kirk recognizes the creature as the one that destroyed half the crew of the U.S.S. Farragut over ten years before, when Kirk was a lieutenant on that vessel. The commander of the Farragut, Captain Garovick, died in that encounter, but his son is now an ensign on the Enterprise. Kirk and Garovick proceed to exorcise their pasts by tracking and destroying the monster.

"Wolf in the Fold" is Robert Bloch's third *Star Trek* episode, adapted from Bloch's story "Yours Truly, Jack the Ripper," which was also adapted, more directly, in a 1961 episode of *Thriller* simply titled "The Ripper." The basic idea is that the Ripper is actually a long-lived being, but this at first is not revealed, as it is Scotty, recovering from a head injury, who is suspected of the horrible murders of several young women. Ultimately, the creature is exposed in its latest human form, and expelled into the depths of space. The phrase "He's dead, Jim" is used here an unsurpassed number of times.

"The Trouble With Tribbles" is a comical episode in which Klingons and furry little creatures that reproduce at an alarming rate threaten the peace on the Enterprise, as well as an important grain shipment. Fortunately, the tribbles that eat the grain reveal that it was poisoned by a Klingon spy, and all ends well, with the Klingons getting stuck with the remaining tribbles. Scotty gets into a brawl with Klingons in this extremely popular episode.

"The Gamesters of Triskelion" are bored aliens who abduct Kirk, Chekov and Uhura to take part in gladiatorial games for their amusement. When the Enterprise, under Spock's command, reaches Triskelion, the ship is captured. Kirk makes a bet with the aliens and is set to fight Shahna, a beautiful woman. He wins the wager when it turns out that he has managed to teach her about human ideals (as well as about kissing), and the ship and crew, as well as the people of the planet, are freed. In an intriguing career move, Angelique Pettijohn, who portrayed Shahna, later went on to star in various "adult" movies.

"A Piece of the Action" is another humorous episode in which Kirk discovers a civilization that has modeled itself on the society described in a book left by a Federation mission one hundred years before: *Chicago Mobs of the Twenties*. Kirk is confounded by this situation until he decides to play along, and soon he and Spock are wearing pinstripes and fedoras and spouting variants of archaic Earth slang. Thus, Kirk finally succeeds in uniting the Iotians into a single government.

"The Immunity Syndrome" brings the Enterprise up against a giant space amoeba which must be destroyed; Spock and McCoy both vie for the chance to observe the creature firsthand in a shuttlecraft, but Spock gets this quite possibly fatal honor. Spock discovers that the creature is about to divide, and destroys it before its threat can be doubled. With life support waning, he barely makes it back to the ship in time.

"A Private Little War" takes place on the planet Neural, where Klingons are providing arms to escalate a tribal conflict preparatory to their own invasion. Kirk must find someone he knew on his last visit to this world, the leader Tyree, but is attacked by a vicious Mugatu, a horned yeti-like being, and becomes ill from its poison. Tyree's wife cures him but steals his phaser, only to be killed by the tribe backed by the Klingons. Tyree, reluctant to fight, now is determined to do so, and Kirk can only leave weapons to help maintain the balance of power on the planet. This was intended as a commentary on the Vietnam War, and was modelled on actual political realities.

"Return to Tomorrow" finds Kirk, Spock and Dr. Anne Mulhall lending their bodies to the disembodied minds of Sargon, Henoch and Thalassa, respectively, who are the sole survivors of their advanced civilization. The loan is intended to last just long enough to construct permanent android hosts. Henoch, however, decides to keep Spock's body, and tries to kill Sargon/Kirk as well as destroying the device holding Spock's displaced mind.

Fortunately these plans are foiled, and everyone gets their bodies back; the beings decide to enjoy life in the universe without benefit of bodies.

This episode gave Nimoy and Shatner some room to act, and featured, as Dr. Mulhall, the first *Star Trek* appearance of actress Diana Muldaur.

"Patterns of Force" features another civilization tampered with by a Federation emissary. In this case it is historian John Gill, who has tried to create an ordered society by using the structure of Nazi Germany. This scheme has backfired, and Gill is drugged and used as a figurehead by Melakon, a very unpleasant fellow. Gill's former history student, James Kirk, and Spock investigate. They're captured, then escape to save yet another addlebrained culture from itself.

"By Any Other Name" ultimately concerns alien spies who assume human form only to be confounded by their own newfound human nature. The Kelvan mission to Federation space hijacks the enterprise preparatory to the three-hundred year journey back to their home world. Kirk, Scotty, Spock and the other crew members not turned into small blocks (!) manage to turn the aliens' passions against them, and the Kelvans give up when they realize that they have become too human to survive on their original planet.

"Omega Glory" features yet another parallel history: the warring Kohms and Yangs parallel the Communists and Yankees of the Vietnam War era. A starship captain has set himself as warlord with the Kohms; Kirk and Spock finally rally the Yangs when Kirk realizes that their sacred words are actually a distortion of the Preamble to the U.S. Constitution! All in all, one of the more heavy-handed episodes of *Star Trek*.

Early in 1968, the volume of mail provoked by Bjo Trimble's letter campaign led the network to announce on the air after the March 1, 1968 broadcast of "Omega Glory" that *Star Trek* would, indeed, be returning in the fall.

A press release soon followed:

UNPRECEDENTED VIEWER REACTION IN SUPPORT OF "STAR TREK" LEADS TO ON-AIR ANNOUNCEMENT OF SERIES' SCHEDULING FOR 1968-69.

In response to unprecedented viewer reaction in support of the continuation of the NBC Television Network's STAR TREK series, plans for continuing the series in the Fall were announced on NBC-TV immediately following last Friday night's episode of the space adventure series. The announcement will be repeated following next Friday's program.

From early December to date, NBC has received 114,667 pieces of mail in support of STAR TREK, and 52,151 in the month of February alone.

Immediately after last Friday night's program, the following announcement was made:

"And now an announcement of interest to all viewers of STAR TREK. We are pleased to tell you that STAR TREK will continue to be seen on NBC Television. We know you will be looking forward to seeing the weekly adventure in space on STAR TREK."

On the regular series front at the time, "The Ultimate Computer" is the brainchild, almost literally, of scientist Richard Daystrom, who programs it with his own brain patterns. Installed on the Enterprise, the M-5 takes command and decimates the crew of another starship when it mistakenly believes that wargames are an actual attack. Ultimately Kirk outsmarts the machine and order is restored.

"Bread and Circuses" takes Kirk and crew to a world with a history parallel to that of Earth, with one exception: this world's equivalent of the Roman Empire has lasted well into the 20th century. (This was undoubtedly very convenient as far as the wardrobe department was concerned.) Captain Merik, a Federation officer, has taken a place of power in this culture, and got rid of his crew by sending them to their deaths in the gladiatorial games.

Kirk, McCoy and Spock seem faced with a similar fate, but Scotty sabotages the planet's power source, enabling them to escape, and a repentant

Merik gives Kirk his communicator before dying. All is well, and as the Enterprise leaves they discover that the underground opposition to the "Romans" seems to be a Christian cult, further reinforcing the parallel history concept.

"Assignment Earth" incorporated the script of a pilot proposed by Roddenberry into the *Star Trek* continuity. Once again, the Enterprise travels through time, this time to 1968. Here they meet Gary Seven (Robert Lansing), a human (supposedly) trained by aliens to defend Earth.

Kirk and Spock follow him to New York. Seven's mission is to prevent the launching of a Star-Wars type orbiting defense system that will actually prove disastrous to humanity. With the help of Roberta Lincoln (Teri Garr) he manages to evade Kirk, but eventually is caught up with; he then manages to convince the captain of the importance of his mission, and the space bomb is destroyed. The story ends with a hint that Seven and Roberta will have more adventures, but a spin-off series never materialized.

Writing in the June 1968 issue of *Variety*, Nimoy stated, "During the first season of *Star Trek* a wise director gave me this advice: 'Build in all the character elements you can find right now while you still have your strength. As time goes on, the attrition will be devastating.' I took his advice and am very grateful for it. The fact is, a great deal of talent is required to work successfully in television—perhaps even more than in features. The finished TV product is nothing more than a series of educated, artistic guesses determined solely by the previous experience of the individuals involved. Time to cogitate, to digest or to live with an idea before committing it to film is strictly forbidden. The very basic form of creativity is undermined. If you'll forgive a tongue-twisting axiom, 'Thesis versus antithesis results in dramatic synthesis. Time and creative energy provide the dramatic content.' Remove the element of time and the synthesis becomes forced and arbitrary, lacking fresh insight." Nimoy went on to reveal that, "On the *Star Trek* set we've actually had rewrites arrive seconds and even minutes after the scene had been shot. Time beats TV by a nose. And the viewers finish out of the money!"

During the between-season break, DeForest Kelley, apparently not the happiest cast member of *Star Trek*, was profiled in TV Guide on August 24, 1968:

Even now, [Kelley's] beachhead seems to him less than entirely secure. "When I see the trade papers, after a whole season, still list only Bill Shatner and Leonard Nimoy as co-stars, I burn a little inside," says De (pronounced Dee) Kelley. "I've had a rough road in this business, and billing can be an actor's life's blood. What I want, as a co-star, is simply to be counted in fully. I've had to fight for everything I've gotten at Star Trek, from a parking space at the studio to an unshared dressing room, and sometimes the patience wears raw. I know that my role is more passive. I know that Bill and Leonard have easier parts to write for. But I've been through episodes where I'm standing there, without a word, for twelve pages of dialogue. Once I got left out of an episode entirely. I went to the writer— he also has producer status on the show— and he said, very apologetically, 'De, I'm sorry, but it was an oversight.' An oversight! If a writer-producer on my own show forgets me, then I've got problems!"

All of this is uttered in a soft Georgia accent— Yankee-ized somewhat now by speech training and sounding remarkably like a testy David Brinkley. Such candor about his grievances, however, runs contrary to De Kelley's usual demeanor as an easy-natured, impeccably mannered, almost placid Southern gentleman. Around the Star Trek lot— ironically the show is filmed at Paramount Studios, where he started out , in his first flick, as a movie star— De Kelley is immensely popular with his fellow actors and crew. He's the one who remembers the birthdays of the technician's children; let a script girl's mother take ill, and Kelley is the first to send flowers. "De really cares about people," says Leonard (Spock) Nimoy. He is truly the most human of all the actors I've ever known," says William (Captain Kirk) Shatner: "There's a simple, unassuming niceness about this man that's rare in any business."

Shortly before his father died, in 1966, Kelley unburdened his thoughts in a long letter. He says: "I told my father that as I look back. remembering how he captivated all of us with his sermons, he was probably the real reason I became an actor. I didn't realize it, but I wanted to be an actor like him. A good preacher, like a good lawyer, is a good actor—and my father was a good preacher."

In some ways De Kelley remains Southern to the core. On New Year's Day he cooks black-eyed peas with red-eyed gravy—for luck in the ensuing year. And he still cherishes small triumphs. When his name ran for the first time this year in a TV Guide crossword puzzle, his wife clipped the page and framed it to hang on the wall. "It's not an Oscar or an Emmy," says De Kelley, "but to an actor it's something.'

Soon afterwards, the Fall Preview of *TV Guide* came out, and had this to say about *Star Trek:*

More hazardous than all their encounters in outer space for the Star Trekkers are those Nielsen ratings, and they just barely eked by with a renewal for this season. Last term, their future was in considerable doubt, and only a heavy mail campaign from avid viewers played an important part in keeping the show on.

Executive producer Gene Roddenberry still was on the verge of quitting the show because they changed its time slot to 10 P.M. Fridays, a time he thinks bodes no good for the future of his series, since it slots the show opposite the movies on CBS and Judd on ABC. But he did agree to remain with it, despite his unhappiness at the change.

Roddenberry tells us that this season the only change is to expose the secondary characters more fully, to give viewers a better idea of their personalities. He remarks of the gang in Trek, "We have the truly multi-racial cast, and in two years we've had only three crank letters." In one of the stories this season, the Trekkers land on a planet identical in physical makeup to Earth. On that planet, police are selected as carefully as we select scientists, and the question is posed: Could our police be better? "We are using science fiction to show the police as they could or should be if they had support from the public, and scientific support," explains ex-cop Roddenberry.

This item was, however, more than a bit premature, as Roddenberry did quit as the producer of *Star Trek*. As suspected, NBC was sneakily shifting its stance with regard to *Star Trek*. They had announced that the show would be aired in a 7:30 PM, prime time slot on Mondays. . . only to turn around and stick *Star Trek* on at 10:00 PM on Friday, a time slot with the stench of certain death. It seemed that *Rowan and Martin's Laugh-In* had a prior claim on that particular time slot. To further compound their infamy, they only contracted for thirteen episodes instead of a full season's worth. (In the end, the series did run a full season one last time.)

Roddenberry planned to put Gene L. Coon in his place, but illness and other commitments kept this from coming about; *Outer Limits* producer Joseph Stefano was invited to step in but declined. Roddenberry was forced to choose someone untested; although his replacements came highly recommended, they were not familiar with the basic ideas and relationships within the series, and were therefore destined to oversee a number of episodes in which the basic integrity of *Star Trek* and its characters were sadly undermined to varying degrees.

CHAPTER FIVE

AN AREA OF TURBULENCE
(The Third and Final Season)

Some years later, DeForest Kelley would reflect on the series' final season. "The third year was not a good year because there was too much going on; problems with the network, thinking we were going to be dropped, bad time slots. A kind of internal revolution took place, so to speak, and it began to show, which we were all very concerned about.

"[Gene Roddenberry] began to slack off in the latter part of the second season because other things enter into what then was thought to be a successful show. Demands began to be put upon his time in other directions and he then, in turn, brought in other people to assist him. The third year he began to battle with NBC over the time slot and he became terribly upset and told them he would not produce the show personally if it were placed in a ten o'clock time slot on Friday night. We had a tremendous university audience and school audience and it would lose viewers if it were on at that time. NBC went ahead and did it and Gene pulled out. They brought another producer in who was not familiar with the show and it began to go downhill."

Indeed, on September 20, 1968, *Star Trek* began its third and final season with what may rightly be considered its single worst episode: "Spock's Brain."

In "Spock's Brain," the object in question is stolen by a beautiful woman who then vanishes. McCoy manages to keep Spock's body going, and they take it with them when they reach the woman's planet. It seems that the brain was needed to run the planet's power system. This computer even speaks with Spock's voice. Eventually the brain is regained, and McCoy uses an alien teaching device to provide him, temporarily, with the knowledge necessary to put the brain back in Spok.

"The Enterprise Incident" sends the Enterprise on what is essentially an espionage mission: Kirk feigns a mental breakdown and takes the ship into the Neutral Zone. Outgunned by Romulans, he is captured, and Spock denounces his actions. McCoy beams to the Romulan ship just as Kirk attacks Spock; Spock kills the captain with the Vulcan Death Grip and the body is beamed back to the Enterprise. Of course, there is no Vulcan Death grip, and Kirk is revived, surgically altered to look like a Romulan, and beamed back to steal the Romulan cloaking device. The Enterprise makes good its escape once Scotty gets the stolen cloaking device installed and working.

Fans, however, were highly critical of the episode for the way Spock acted out of character; D.C. Fontana bore the brunt of the blame for this for a time, until it was revealed that her original story had been rewritten by other hands.

"The Paradise Syndrome" strands an amnesiac Kirk on a planet while the Enterprise must seek and destroy an asteroid headed directly for that world. The attempt fails and the damaged ship heads back at sublight speed. In the months that this takes, Kirk is hailed as a God by the American Indian-like natives of the planet. He falls in love with a priestess and marries her.

Meanwhile, Spock deciphers the inscriptions on an obelisk near Kirk's home and discovers that it is a device to deflect asteroids. Kirk and his wife are supposed to know how to activate it; when they can't, the people stone them. Spock arrives just in time to set off the device, saving the planet, but Kirk's pregnant wife dies from her injuries.

"And the Children Shall Lead" involves the children on a scientific outpost, whose parents all committed suicide. The kids are under the influence of "the friendly angel" Gorgan, in truth an evil entity; the ship is threatened but Gorgan's aims are thwarted when the children remember their parents and turn against him.

"Is There In Truth No Beauty?" is the question posed when a Medusan comes on board; this race cannot be looked upon by humanoid eyes. Kolos, who stays in a protective case, is accompanied by the telepathic Dr. Miranda Jones. Marvick, an engineer on board, has been in love with Jones for years, and is driven by jealousy to try to kill Kolos.

The sight of the alien drives him mad, and he goes, crazed, to engineering and casts the ship into strange uncharted regions of space. The Medusan's amazing navigational powers are the only hope; Spock performs a mind meld wearing protective eyeglasses, but forgets them and is driven mad, too, after the ship is saved. Jones,

who is revealed to be blind, must overcome her own jealous attachment to Kolos in order to help Spock.

This marks the second Star Trek appearance of Diana Muldaur, who plays Miranda Jones.

"Spectre of the Gun" hurls Kirk and crew into a deadly simulation of the gunfight at the O.K. Corral. Only by accepting it as an illusion can they survive. But only by refusing to kill can they prove to the Melkotians, who put them there, that they deserve their place in the universe.

"The Day of the Dove" pits the Federation crew against Klingons. All at the machinations of a being that feeds off of hostile and violent emotions. When the Klingons are captured and taken on board, the alien turns phasers into swords, and battles ensue. The wounded are healed to fight again. Kirk eventually convinces the Klingon commander, Kang, that they must work together, and they put on a convincing show of friendship that drives the evil being away.

"For The World Is Hollow and I Have Touched The Sky" concerns the world of Yonanda. The people there are controlled by the Oracle and don't realize that their planet is actually a space ship. Yonanda is headed for a disastrous collision with a giant asteroid. A landing crew beams down, including Dr. McCoy, who has learned that he has an incurable terminal disease. He falls in love with the high priestess and is prepared to stay with her. Kirk and Spock manage to reach the Oracle computer's memory banks, and obtain information that will save Yonanda. . . and cure McCoy, who bids a wistful farewell to his new flame.

In "The Tholian Web," The Enterprise discovers a dead ship which seems to be drifting into another dimension. When the survey crew returns, Kirk is stranded on the ship when it disappears. His air supply is limited, and rescue efforts are hindered by the fact that the area of space causes humans to act aggressively towards each other. Kirk's ghostly figure, caught in an interdimensional limbo, begins appearing to the crew at intervals. The Tholians, an unknown race, show up, accuse the Federation of trespassing, and begin to spin the web of the title. Spock eludes them, and Kirk is rescued just in the nick of time.

"Plato's Stepchildren" are the inhabitants of Platonius, who have great telekinetic powers but have no immunity to disease. When McCoy beams down to help them, he, along with Kirk and Spock, is subjected to their cruel whims. Nurse Chapel and Uhura are drawn into these humiliations; Spock is forced to sing. Alexander, a powerless dwarf, tries to help them but cannot. Finally, McCoy figures out that the powers of the Platonians derive from a chemical in their systems. With this knowledge, he is able to duplicate those power for himself and his fellow crewmen. They escape, and free Alexander from his malicious masters. This episode is notable for having featured television's first interracial kiss, as Kirk and Uhura are forced to kiss by the malicious superbeings.

"Wink of an Eye" describes the condition of the Scalosians, whose radioactive water has sped up their life-rate so fast that they can only be perceived as a buzzing noise. When Kirk takes some of this water, he can perceive them, but his crew cannot sense him. The Scalosians plan to use him to repopulate their world. McCoy devise an antidote but Spock must first take some water and be sped up himself in order to find and save the Captain.

"The Empath" is Gem, a beautiful mute woman. Kirk and McCoy are kidnapped and tortured by aliens; Gem is an empath who can absorb their pain and injuries, healing the terrible agonies inflicted on them. McCoy's injuries threaten to kill him, but she prevents this, risking her own life. This cruel test turns out to have a humane motivation, of sorts: two planets are threatened by an imminent disaster, but the aliens can only save the inhabitants of one, and have been trying to determine which race is more worthy of survival.

"Elaan of Troyius" is on the Enterprise on her way to a diplomatically advantageous marriage, but she's more interested in Kirk; when she cries, the touch of her tears chemically induce Kirk to fall in love with her. Klingons confound matters, but all works out when Elaan's jewels turn out to be dilithium crystals. Kirk ultimately breaks free of her spell and she proceeds with her important mission.

"Whom Gods Destroy" takes place on a planetary asylum for the last group of mentally ill people in human society. Kirk brings a new drug that can cure these last vestiges of madness, but the asylum has been taken over by a shape-changing madman, who tries to steal the Enterprise by taking Kirk's form. The astute Mr. Spock manages to determine which is the real Jim and saves the day.

"Let That Be Your Last Battlefield" tackles prejudice by reducing it to absurdity. Lokai, late of the planet Cheron, is half black and half white, being neatly bisected, pigmentwise, right down the middle. When he shows up on the Enterprise, he is pursued by Bele, who looks exactly the same. . .except that his coloration makes him a mirror image of Lokai. This left/right distinction has been the root of hatred on their home world for generations. When the Enterprise finally reaches Cheron, after nearly being demolished by the battles between the two passengers, it is revealed to be completely dead. Lokai and Cheron beam down to their world to continue their ancient, pointless conflict to their deaths.

In "The Mark of Gideon," Kirk seems to disappear while beaming down. . . at least from the perspective of the bridge. Kirk, on the other hand, finds himself on the bridge completely alone, with no trace of Spock or the others. This is in fact an exact replica of the real Enterprise. Kirk has been kidnapped because the people of Gideon, free from all disease, are suffering from overpopulation. Kirk, having survived one deadly disease, still carries it, and the plan is to use him to introduce disease back into the world of Gideon. Spock manages to find and rescue him, but not before this new vector has been unleashed on Gideon.

"That Which Survives" is the holographic image of a beautiful woman; the projection's touch is fatal. Designed to keep other races away from the artifacts of a long-dead civilization, she costs several lives, and nearly gets Mr. Sulu before Spock manages to pull the plug on the ancient computer.

"The Lights of Zetar" are the disembodied survivors of Zetar, who seek a host in which to continue their existence. They settle on Lt. Mira Romaine, an officer supervising the transfer of the Federation's records to a new library facility. They possess her, which seriously hampers the possibility of romance between her and Scotty. The Lights are finally driven out when Mira enters a pressure chamber.

"Requiem for Methuselah" takes Kirk and crew to Holberg 917-G in search of the antidote to a deadly disease. There they encounter a Mr. Flint and Reena, a beautiful young lady, and Kirk falls for her right off the bat. Eventually it is discovered that Flint is actually an immortal who lived on Earth for centuries; among his aliases were Da Vinci and Brahms. But without Earth's atmosphere to preserve him, his immortality is nearing its end. Reena is the last of a series of androids he has constructed to keep him company. This bothers Kirk more than a bit, so Spock obligingly clears Kirk's mind of the unhappy memory.

"The Way To Eden" is sought by the charismatic but crazed Dr. Sevrin and his youthful disciples, who could only be described as space hippies. One of them is an old flame of Chekov's, and he tries to understand her new interests but just can't get the swing of it.

Kirk must give the seekers free reign of his ship, orders due to the presence of an important diplomat's son among them. Ultimately, Sevrin incapacitates the bridge crew and steals a shuttle.

He and his followers find Eden, a truly beautiful planet, but everything about it is toxic. Sevrin and one young man die before the others can be rescued. The original version of this script included Dr. McCoy's daughter Joanna among the young seekers, but she was dropped, and in fact never appeared in the series despite several planned attempts to feature her as a character.

"The Cloud Minders" dwell in the skyborne city of Stratos; the Troglodytes live on the surface of Ardana, excavating zienite for the benefit of their social superiors. When Kirk arrives seeking zienite, needed to resolve a crisis on another world, he cannot avoid getting entangled in this inequitable situation.

He eventually resolves this situation by intentionally trapping himself and leaders of both classes in a mine shaft, where the Troglodytes' alleged inferiority and brutality is demonstrated to be merely an effect of gasses in the mines. Kirk leaves with the zienite, sure in the knowledge that social reforms are finally underway.

In "The Savage Curtain" the Enterprise is hailed by Abraham Lincoln, who just happens to be floating in space nearby. Kirk and Spock follow the dead president to the lava-ridden surface of a nearby planet. Yarnek, a stone creature desirous of understanding the concepts of ":good' and "evil', pits them, along with Vulcan philosopher Surak, against Genghis Khan, a notorious Klingon, a killer from Earth's past and a famous bloodthirsty criminal. A philosophical slugfest, where the main question is: if Yarnek doesn't know good from evil. . . how does he know who to put on which side?!?

"All Our Yesterdays" involves another time portal through which Kirk, Spock and McCoy pass. This one is located on the planet Sarpeidon, whose people have fled an impending nova by relocating to various different periods in their past history. Kirk goes through first and winds up in an era similar to Reformation England, where he is in danger of being killed as a witch.

Spock and the doctor find themselves in a prehistoric ice age, where the Vulcan reverts to his ancestors' lustful ways and becomes involved with a woman, Zarabeth. They believe that they cannot return to their temporal starting point without dying, but this is not actually true as they did not undergo the necessary treatments. Meanwhile, Kirk resolves his troubles with the help of another time traveller, and manages to reclaim his friends and get back to the ship just before the nova destroys the planet.

"Turnabout Intruder", the final *Star Trek* episode to be filmed, was dubbed "Captain Kirk, Space Queen" by the crew. Here, a woman once spurned by Kirk in favor of his Starfleet career gets her revenge by switching bodies with him and and taking over his ship! Spock determines the truth of this by using a Vulcan mind meld on Dr. Janice Lester's body, but has a hard time convincing anyone that Kirk's body is occupied by a woman.

Eventually, McCoy is brought in on this, only to be accused of mutiny along with Spock, and sentenced to death. By this point, everyone realizes that something is drastically amiss, and Kirk shakes off the effects of the mind transfer.

A rather intriguing acting chore, this role was apparently enlivened by William Shatner's off-camera gags. In one scene, when McCoy examines Kirk, Shatner slipped off a hospital robe to reveal plastic breasts. Unperturbed, DeForest Kelley stayed in character, leading Shatner to break up into hysterical laughter. Needless to say, this never made it into the final cut. Shatner, perhaps obsessed with the theme of this episode, later appeared on set in full drag. Later in the shooting, however, Shatner came down with a vicious case of the flu, but still kept up his shooting schedule.

Final word of *Star Trek* 's cancellation came through during this shooting; when "Turnabout Intruder" wrapped, it was a wrap for *Star Trek* as well. If the network had ordered the last few shows ready to go, Shatner would have made his debut as director with the very next episode.

"Turnabout Intruder" was also the last *Star Trek* episode to be aired; it was broadcast on June 3, 1969. In August, when the final network rerun aired, it was "Requiem For Methuselah" and the last word spoken was by Spock, who said, "Forget. . . "

But many would not.

SPOTLIGHT ON THE CIA
What Role Did Casey Play?

Newsweek.

December 22, 1986 · $2.00

The Enduring
Power of
STAR
TREK

Leonard Nimoy
as Mr. Spock

CHAPTER SIX:

MOVING THROUGH LIMBO AND BEYOND

(The Lost Years. . . to Star Trek:The Motion Picture)

Although to the casual observer it might have seemed that Gene Roddenberry's brainchild was dead and buried, this was not the case. The Seventies were actually the decade when national interest in *Star Trek* began to build at an incredible rate. Already having a strong base of support, it could only draw more fans than ever as the series began to repeat again and again in syndication. As early as 1972, *TV Guide* made note of this:

All over the country today, people are wearing "Star Trek Lives"

T-shirts, pasting Mr. Spock bumper stickers on their cars and maybe, for all I know, falling on their knees before graven images of Mr. Spock.

Why? Well, it's because, back at the end of January, Star Trek's fanatic band of followers held their first national convention— nearly three years after the series was shot out of orbit by NBC.

" We ran into Shirley Gerstel of Paramount Television, which had provided 13 Star Trek episodes to be screened at the convention. "The calls and letters that come into my office are tremendous," she told us. "I keep passing them on to the West Coast. I never thought that Star Trek would come back, but now there's a rumor that Paramount might start making it again."

That, indeed, was the convention's principal rumor; it passed from one Trekkie to another, electrifying them. We asked Gene Roddenberry, Star Trek's executive producer and creator, and the convention's guest of honor, about the rumor of Star Trek's return.

"I didn't think it was possible six months ago," he said a little dazedly, "but after seeing the enthusiasm here, I'm beginning to change my mind. It is possible to do it from my standpoint. We had such a family group on the show that it's totally different for us. We still meet and drink together, and we're all still friends, so for this show it is possible." (Someone else added darkly that the Green Acres crew did not still meet and drink together.)

In 1973, *Star Trek* finally returned to the airwaves. . . as a Saturday morning, animated cartoon series. Although Leonard Nimoy seemed less than enthusiastic about the idea, he signed on to provide Spock's voice. Interviewed by the L.A. Free Press before work on the cartoon had actually begun, he sighed when asked about it; he wasn't certain that the new series wouldn't reduce *Star Trek* to an idiotic piece of juvenilia:

That's why I sigh. We don't know. Unfortunately, I don't have control over the material. I will have control only to the extent that I can refuse to do a script that is sent to me, and then I am in breach of contract, and we start with that whole business again.

I was in Florida when this thing came up and I was contacted by mail and by phone. It was very difficult. All the people who were doing it were here in California, and I was assured by all, my agent and Gene Roddenberry and Dorothy Fontana, who's going to produce the show, that the intention was to do a very special kind of animation, to really use the medium properly and successfully and to maintain the quality that Star Trek originally was intended to have. And, that the material would be new, fresh, good stuff. We were really going to do it right.

O.K. Everybody starts out with good intentions. I have never met a producer or a writer who came to me and said, "We are going to do something that is going to be so lousy. . ." Nobody ever says that. I believe that these people mean it. But when the exigencies set in, they start to turn out some scripts. They take them to [the] people who are financing it and they say, "Oh, wait a minute, we can't do this, I mean, this script would be terrific for a philosophy department at UCLA, but not for a Saturday morning cartoon television. It won't work."

Then the arguments start. And it's a question of how tough they're going to be and how strong they're going to be in taking a stand on what is good Star Trek.

The rest of the cast reprised their roles as well, with the exception of Walter Koenig, who kept his hand in with a script. Two new alien characters were added; James Doohan and Majel Barrett did extra duty, providing the voices for the new characters as well as most of the supporting cast as well.

DeForest Kelley (in the Gulick interview) noted that Roddenberry's involvement with the animated series faded somewhat after a strong beginning:

. . .Dorothy Fontana was really running that show. Because it is so dependent on artists, there was not much Gene could do except see to it that above-average scripts were sent in for it. And you'll notice that most of the scripts were not written for children. They are adult scripts and some of them are very good, and would have made good [live-action] Star Treks.

I did two animated shows here in Lubbock [Texas, where Kelley was appearing in the play Beginner's luck at the time of this interview] a couple of weeks ago. To do those two scripts took me a little over an hour because I gave four or five readings of each line. In case they didn't like the way I read a line, I'd read it three or four more times, so they could pick the one they wanted. It was a little bit time consuming.

At the time, there was some thought that the animated series might serve as the first in the necessary series of events needed to get a live action *Star Trek* back on the air in prime time. Again, DeForest Kelley:

That was Gene's thought, I think. I questioned it at the time he said he was going to do it, as I thought it was the death blow. Gene said, "No, I don't feel that way at all. I think it's important to keep some form of Star Trek alive and in the minds of people.

It's not the network, Kelley pointed out, that was keeping the series from being revived. The network wants the show again and would love to have it back. But Paramount, the studio which owns Star Trek, doesn't want to make Star Trek prime time because they're making so much money in syndication with it. They feel they would be competing with themselves.

As far as a "real" Star Trek revival, Kelley was ready and willing to dust off Dr. McCoy's medical diploma and 23rd Century medical tools.

I would go with it if everybody else went with it. I think if the whole cast was pulled together again it would be nice.

It was a very satisfying show to do because it was such a loved show.

I think we all feel that way. But we now know the tremendous impact that it has made and is still making. It is rather a delight to be associated with it, even though it's been a mixed blessing for me. I think it's hurt my career. I didn't realize that until the last couple of years. I found myself so identified with it and the identification has grown stronger over the years. If Star Trek doesn't renew itself, it is my job to break that identification and get back into what I was doing, or something else.

I believe the popularity of Star Trek is stronger than it has ever been. It will, in my opinion, be very difficult to ever have another show that has created the kind of feeling that Star Trek has created. I doubt very seriously if there will ever be another one. It was a one-of-a-kind thing.

The idea for the animated series was pitched to Gene Roddenberry by Lou Scheimer and Norm Prescott of Filmation, one of the higher quality television animation studios; although not fully animated, their productions had more movement that the average Saturday morning fodder.

Roddenberry was swayed by their intention to honor the shows dignity and its original ideals; no cute kids or anthropomorphic canines would be added to the Enterprise crew. Scripts were provided by numerous *Star Trek* alumni: David Gerrold (author of "The Trouble With Tribbles,") Samuel Peeples (who wrote the second *Star Trek* pilot) and Marc Daniels (who directed fourteen episodes of the original series) were all contributing writers.

Unfortunately, despite its noble intentions, the animated *Star Trek* came across generally stiff and lifeless. The animation was partly at fault here, and the new characters were merely visual additions with no real personalities. Some of the writing, such as Walter Koenig's "The Infinite Vulcan" script (which involved giant Spock clones!) left a great deal to be desired.

Rehashes of bizarre aging diseases and tribbles (this time they grew to immense size— a recurring theme?) did little to make the project a fountainhead of originality. The fact that the cast recorded their parts at different locations around the country did little to help recreate the original feeling of camaraderie of the original series, and in fact the actors often came across as though they were merely reciting lines rather than interacting with their fellow cast members.

One of the animated *Star Trek*'s twenty-two episodes, however, is worthy of some further comment: "Yesteryear," by D.C. Fontana, who wrote "Journey To Babel" for the live-action series. This story, featuring the Guardian of Forever from "The City On The Edge Of Forever" (voiced this time by James Doohan, who worked overtime on this series), involves Spock's journey through time back to his childhood on Vulcan, which has somehow caused some sort of time distortion.

He encounters himself at the point during his youth when he was torn between his human and Vulcan heritages; the dramatic focus of the story is the death of his pet sehlet,

I-Chaya (mentioned in "Journey To Babel"). The network (again, NBC) wanted a happy ending, as the death of a pet, they feared, would upset young viewers, but Fontana fought for her original drama and won. She expressed her feelings on this issue a year later in a fanzine article:

I-Chaya's death was absolutely necessary to the story. Part of Spock's training had to do with the facing of responsibilities and realities. One of the greatest weaknesses of children's programming on television, especially animation, is the presentation of total non-reality. Things do die— plants, pets and people. Is there anyone who, as a child, has not suffered the loss of a pup? In that deciding that I-Chaya should die with peace and dignity rather than pain and suffering, young Spock accepted reality and responsibility.

Unfortunately, D.C. Fontana's thoughtful and sensitive script was her only contribution to the animated *Star Trek,* and the series soon faded out and away. Interestingly, Alan Dean Foster wrote a *Star Trek Log* series of paperbacks that served much the same purposes for the cartoon series as the late James Blish's prose adaptations did for the original show; Foster wove the stories together in each volume, often adding to them the depth that was sadly missing from the episodes themselves. The animated *Star Trek* ran during the 1973 and 1974 television seasons; they are now available on home video cassettes.

Another indication of *Star Trek*'s undying popularity came to light on September 19, 1974, which was Star Trek Day at the Movieland Wax Museum in Buena Park, California. Unveiled to the public that day, in response to the frequent requests found in the museum's suggestion box, was a replica of the U.S.S. Enterprise bridge, occupied by lifelike wax representations of Kirk, Spock, McCoy and Uhura. (Scotty, Sulu and Chekov would be added to the display in 1978.)

Sculpted by Lia de Lio and detailed by Logan Fleming, these uncannily realistic figures made quite an impression on their real life counterparts who were in attendance at the gala opening:William Shatner, Nichelle Nichols, DeForest Kelley and Leonard Nimoy. Also in attendance were Gene Roddenberry and wife Majel Barrett, who was not represented in the display.

In 1975, the *Tomorrow Show* hosted by Tom Snyder featured guests DeForest Kelley, James Doohan, Walter Koenig and Harlan Ellison. They discussed the enduring popularity of Star Trek and the rumors of a revival as a feature film. It was a very windy hour, but among the more interesting comments were those of Walter Koenig who commented:

The only problem is, if [Star Trek]'s a feature film as opposed to a made-for-television show, they'll decide that they have to change the thrust of it in some way, make it monsters and huge battle scenes; something that you can't get on television. You may distort the entire feeling of the show.

Time would prove Koenig to be absolutely correct.

Finally, in 1975, Paramount Pictures announced its intention to provide a budget of two to three million dollars for a *Star Trek* film, if Roddenberry could provide a script that suited them. His initial submission, in which the Enterprise and its crew met God (or an entity calling itself God, a fine semantical and theological distinction, as the late Philip K. Dick once observed), seemed a bit too outre for the studio, so they began to look at scripts from other sources.

John D. F. Black submitted an outline, as did Theodore Sturgeon, Robert Silverberg and even Ray Bradbury. Harlan Ellison's encounter with a dimwitted producer who insisted that Ellison's proposed story would be acceptable only if it was reworked to include ancient Mayans (the man had been reading Von Daniken, it seems) is legendary.

In the midst of this constant hunt for a marketable script, DeForest Kelley commented, rather drily, that what Paramount was really looking for was "*Jaws* in space."

Also in 1975, Leonard Nimoy released an autobiographical book with what was, to some *Star Trek* aficionados, an ominous (if not downright sinister) title, *I Am Not Spock*.

The book was in fact a well-balanced look at an actor's life and career, examining Nimoy's work and focussing on his relationship with the character that made him famous. In some humorous passages, Nimoy actually engages in imaginary conversations with Spock, on a variety of subjects; at some points the similarities between the two personas outweighed the differences.

Basically, the book attempts (and succeeds admirably) to get across the fact that Nimoy exited independently of, and in fact before, the character with whom he is associated. It does not demean the character or *Star Trek* in any way.

In fact, it celebrates the possibilities that *Star Trek* introduced into Nimoy's life after nearly two decades of struggle for work and recognition. The cover featured a shadowy photograph of Nimoy, still wearing his Spock haircut and giving the Vulcan salute; the ears are obscured, leaving their actual contours to the viewer's imagination.

The cover was also available from the publisher (Celestial Arts) as a poster bearing the greeting "Live long and prosper." This was certainly not the work of a man who hated the role that had been more than simply his bread and butter.

And yet, some fans, whose lives seemed to hinge on a *Star Trek* revival, chose to view Nimoy's choice of title as an affront, and an indication that he was cruelly planning to deprive them of their favorite entertainment— if that is an adequate word to describe their sometimes mindless devotion to the series.

If this seems an unfair description of some *Star Trek* fans, bear in mind that it only describes an extreme fringe element, and consider this excerpt from a letter received by Leonard Nimoy some time after the publication of *I Am Not Spock*:

*Good for you. Do not return to Star Trek. I approve your pretensions to stardom. I look forward to your wrecking the greatest show of all time with your ******* tactics. Big man, big money, big book. I Am Not Spock. Really fantastic. We all will cheer when you and your fellow star William Shatner gut the Enterprise of her captain and executive officer.*

*Why the hell should the ******* series go on now if you're going to kick it in the groin before production starts? You and your 'career' can take two running steps straight into hell. We made you and we will unmake you. so you're not Spock, huh? The one, the only slimy character of the Sixties to be put in the Hall of Fame of video along with Matt Dillon and Lucy Ricardo when everything else about television is lost to memory fifty years ago, the one bloody character that became an icon to a generation. i got news for you, as long as you live, you will only be known as Spock, Vulcan hero to a planet of youth. i hereby put a curse on your miserable future career. May 100 million hands turn dials when you appear on the TV screen.*

If this belows and confused correspondence seems a unique case, consider that renowned writer Harlan Ellison once had one of his public speaking engagements disrupted by a young woman who took exception to his assertion that he had written the words spoken by Spock in "City On The Edge Of Forever." Bursting into hysterics, she was appalled that anyone could say such a horrible things, as to her Spock was terribly real, and not a fictional creation of other minds.

Fortunately, the bulk of Star *Trek* fans are well balanced individuals attracted by Roddenberry's message of a hopeful, positive future, in many cases highly trained professional people, and not the handful of unrepresentative, deranged basket cases that have just been discussed.

In a 1976 wire service interview, Roddenberry candidly revealed his own constant surprise at the widespread fervor surrounding his famous creation:

"Sometimes I wish I could walk out the door and leave Star Trek behind," says Gene Rodden-

berry., the man who created the television series and steered it through 79 episodes.

It is not that he has any less affection for his creation. He simply worries that the Starship Enterprise and its voyagers will take over his life. "I'm not a guru and I don't want to be," he says. "It frightens me when I learn of 10,00 people treating a Star Trek script as if it were scripture."

As to the Star Trek conventions: "I have to limit myself to one in the East and one in the West each year. I'm not a performer and frankly those conventions scare the hell out of me.

"It is scary to be surrounded by a thousand people asking questions as if the events in the series actually happened. I'm just afraid that if it goes too far and it appears that I have created a philosophy at answer all human ill that someone will stand up and cry "Fraud!" And with good reason."

"I expect that if the feature turns out well, Paramount will try to bring Star Trek back to television. I would hope that it would take the form of occasional films in the long form. I don't think I could face the insanity of another weekly Star Trek."

Eventually, Paramount pulled the plug on the feature film idea, and *Star Trek* fell back into its all-too-familiar limbo.

In an August 1977 interview, William Shatner expressed his feelings on this latest setback (this is one commentary not likely to appear in any of Paramount's official *Star Trek* histories):

"I feel that it was an idiotic decision by the people at Paramount. A Star Trek feature would be both an entertainment and financial success and its blockage stands as one of the greatest monuments to stupidity.

"As far as I know the movie has been finally cancelled and, in the light of the success of Star Wars, I just can't understand it."

In fact, the surprise success of *Star Wars* may very well have *been* the reason for the turnaround; Paramount couldn't see the success of George Lucas' film as anything other than an unduplicatable, one-shot fluke.

Later in,1977, plans were finally launched for a proposed new series, to be entitled *Star Trek II*. Apparently, now Paramount envisioned itself as being the force behind a "fourth network," a preposterous enough seeming idea at the time which never came to fruition— until years later, when the Fox Network proved this to be a viable concept after all. (Ironically, when a new syndicated *Star Trek* series finally made it to the airwaves in 1987, it would generally be carried on a Fox station in most markets— although not always, as the network itself would have no connection with the show's production.)

Roddenberry pulled a treatment out of his files entitled "Robot's Return," which had been intended for his series *Genesis II,* which never made it beyond the pilot stage (CBS went for the *Planet of the Apes* TV series instead). This story involved the return of an ancient satellite to Earth, a satellite which has gained sentience and seeks its creator, a being called NASA. This, strongly reminiscent of Nomad in "The Changeling," would be the focus of *Star Trek II'* s first episode.

Roddenberry gave the treatment to Alan Dean Foster, the noted science fiction author, who turned it into a *Star Trek* story with one notable difference: instead of Spock, the science officer on the Enterprise bridge is one Lieutenant Xon (known briefly and rather generically as Lieutenant Vulcan), as Leonard Nimoy seemed quite possibly to be unavailable for his role as Spock. The remaining principals had signed; in fact, Nimoy had no problems with returning to the role of Spock, but was holding out in order to resolve his long-standing royalties dispute with Paramount Pictures.

They had made millions of dollars from merchandise— toys, lunchboxes, books and the like— which bore his likeness, and he had not received so much as a single penny from all these revenues.

Meanwhile, actor David Gautreaux was cast as Xon, and Persis Khambatta was signed to play a new character, the exotic and alluring (not to mention hairless) Ilia. A third character, Commodore Decker, was not cast.

Writing proceeded apace, and the "Robot's Return" treatment was developed into a script , "In

Thy Image," by Harold Livingston and Robert Goodwin. Other scripts were also written: "Kitumba," by John Meredyth Lucas; "Deadlock," by David Ambrose; "Tomorrow and the Stars" by Larry Alexander; "The Savage Syndrome," by Margaret Armen and Alf Harris; "The Child," by John Povill and Jaron Summers; "Home," by Worley Thorne; "Home," by Theodore Sturgeon; and "Devil's Due," by Bill Lansford.

As preproduction for *Star Trek II* proceeded apace, plans also developed to make the pilot film something special that could be marketed as a theatrical release in Europe.

Things then began to pick up. The fourth network idea looked like a potential washout, so Paramount decided to go full-bore and convert the television project into a theatrical release. Furthermore, the success of Steven Spielberg's *Close Encounters of the Third Kind* seemed a solid enough refutation of their initial view of *Star Wars* as a fluke; obviously, the public would spend its hard-earned money to attend science fiction films. The bottom line, as always, was cold, hard cash.

The director of *Star Trek: The Motion Picture* was to be Robert Wise, director of the classic *The Day The Earth Stood Still*, which had starred Michael Rennie and Patricia Neal.

Star Trek: The Motion Picture appeared at last in December 1979.

Anticipation was great; rumors that Kirk and the crew met God still persisted from some years earlier, but were disproven by the final product itself.

The story developed from the old "Robot's Return" story treatment had reached its final stage.

In the opening sequence, three Klingon cruisers find themselves faced with a new and unknown alien force which proves resistant to all attacks; the Klingons are utterly destroyed by the thing's energy field. A Federation space station observes these events and relays the information, along with the news that the destructive object is headed directly for Earth.

Spock is introduced on his home planet of Vulcan, where he is attempting to shed his human emotions for good through a difficult Vulcan ceremony known as the Kolinahr. He fails but senses that there is something that may help him in his quest to purge his emotions.

On Earth, Kirk is introduced; he is now an Admiral. He is somewhat annoyed by the fact that his new science officer, the Vulcan Commander Sonak, is not yet on board the new Enterprise, and orders the Vulcan to report to him on the ship within an hour. He then beams up to a dry-dock and meets Mr. Scott; as the Enterprise's transporters are not yet on line, they take a shuttle pod over to the ship.

Kirk explains the new threat to Earth, which of course means that Scotty must again break all records and get an impossible task done in an impossible time. The pod tours the exterior of the new Enterprise, a slow and awestruck special effects shot that showcases Douglas Trumbull's work admirably.

Kirk then meets Uhura, Chekov and Sulu, all ranked as Commanders now; Captain Decker, the Captain of the new ship, learns that Kirk is taking over his command due to the new crisis, which is right up Kirk's line of experience (plus being a challenge for his ego). Decker takes this someone testily, rating a rebuke from Kirk. A transporter malfunction results in the death of Commander Sonak.

The crew then witnesses the destruction of the space outpost by the strange phenomenon they are destined to investigate. Lieutenant Ilia beams aboard without incident; she seems to have had a relationship with Decker on her home planet. Her people are supposedly so sexually charged that she has taken a vow of celibacy for the duration of her Starfleet service..

Dr. McCoy has to be goaded into beaming up, since he hates transporters; he appears, bearded and surly, but he's really glad to be back.

When the Enterprise heads out and goes into warp, it is caught in a wormhole distortion which causes time to slow and space to bend. After a threatening asteroid is destroyed by photon torpedos, everything returns to normal, and the problem with the warp drive is attended to.

In private, McCoy challenges Kirk and accuses him of competing with Decker for command of the ship. Then, an unknown shuttlecraft with Federation registration hails the ship; it is Spock,

who volunteers his services as science officer. Spock is even more aloof than ever. Later he explains that he has sensed an immensely powerful pattern of perfect logic, and hopes that this alien force will be able to help him achieve Kolinahr.

Shortly afterward, the being attacks, and Spock discovers that it is trying to communicate. He makes mental contact with it and the attack ceases as a result. As the ship enters the cloud-like perimeter of the phenomenon, a probe appears on the bridge and whisks Ilia away.

Later, a probe which is an exact duplicate of Ilia appears on board the vessel and observes the crew, describing the humans as 'carbon based units' which infest the ship. Decker tries to find mutual memories in the duplicate Ilia's mind.

Meanwhile, Spock, intent on discovering the true nature of what the imitation Ilia calls Vejur, steals a thruster suit and heads further into the cloud. Attempting a mind meld with the entity, he is overwhelmed by the vastness of its knowledge. Unconscious, he drifts back, to be rescued by Kirk. Spock reveals that he has seen that the pure logic he has aspired to, as realized by Vejur, is empty and cold; his human side, he realizes now, is an important part of him, as he even laughs, and reasserts his friendship with Kirk.

The Vejur entity creates a human-habitable atmosphere outside the Enterprise, and Kirk, McCoy, Spock, Decker and the duplicate Ilia go forth to discover the amazing (if oddly familiar) truth about Vejur: it is a 20th Century space probe (what, again?), Voyager 18, transformed in its centuries of wanderings into a sentient being seeking its creator.

Attempts to explain the truth about NASA and Voyager to the entity fail when it shuts down its receiving components. Spock reasons that if a human could join with the entity, it might understand its link with humanity better, and cease to be a threat. Decker and the Ilia simulation merge with the Vejur craft in a dazzling display of special effects technology, and ascend to a higher level of being. The threat is averted, and the Enterprise resumes its course, apparently in search of new missions.

The problem with this movie was its slow, ponderous development; its all-too awestruck reverence for its own special effects (which are beautifully done— but frequently all too static), and most of all for the short shrift it gives to its own characters' relationships with each other. In essence, the film is too clinical and dispassionate to engage the emotions.

In scenes cut from the theatrical release but restored on video, this is somewhat less the case; each character has his moments. Here, Spock actually weeps after his mind meld with Vejur. Why these scenes were cut remain a mystery. Another restored scene, showing a space suited Kirk emerging from a cargo bay, is notable for the fact that no special effects were ever cued into it; the viewer can see, briefly, the soundstage structure behind him.

Leonard Nimoy had this to say about *Star Trek: The Motion Picture:*

I think we should say, in deference to the people who made the first Star Trek motion picture that they had a very special set of problems. For example, there had not been a Star Trek project for eleven years. We finished making the series in 1968 and here we were in 1979, coming together to do a different Star Trek project. That meant that a lot of very special circumstances had to be addressed. Ground had to be broken in a special kind of way. Do you make comment in the film that eleven years has passed and therefore things have changed? The ship has changed, the uniform has changed, the sets have changed, rank has changed, relationships have changed. We were faced with the concern that we should not be perceived as a blown-up television episode, but should be looked upon as a motion picture. therefore there were certain changes that were expected by the audience, and they must be addressed.

However one looks at it, the final result was a bit pallid. An alternative ending, devised by Douglas Trumbull cohort Mike Minor, was rejected as too costly; the film had already gone way over budget to make its December 7, 1979 release date.

One Paramount executive dubbed the production a "thirty-five million dollar turkey," but cost estimates actually may make that figure another ten million higher; the film grossed one hundred and five million dollars in the United States. The scuttled ending featured the Enterprise being ejected from Vejur, followed by the three Klin-

gon ships from the start of the movie; a battle royale was to ensue, in which the triumphant but damaged Enterprise was to be obliged to undergo a saucer separation— and idea that would eventually turn up elsewhere.

Supposedly, director Robert Wise was unhappy with the final cut of the film; Paramount vetoed any re-editing in order to make the all-important release date. People who attended the Washington, D.C. premiere of the feature reported observing Wise burying his face in his hands at various points in the film, obviously embarrassed.

Roddenberry's novelization of the script contains just the sort of background information and human interest that the film sorely needed.

Kirk, it seems, was semi-retired, involved with a woman who was also using him as a public relations figurehead for Starfleet; Kirk, based in San Francisco, spent his off years lecturing extensively about his space adventures. The person who dies in the transporter accident with Sonak was actually the woman in Kirk's life, a detail left out of the film.

Also in the novel: Ilia's potent sexual chemistry has a clear effect on Sulu, as he becomes physically aroused in her presence. Again, the scene reveals a lot about both characters, but never made it to the screen, not even in the video restoration. So, although the video release provides the opportunity to see *Star Trek: The Motion Picture* at its best, the film remains a fairly disappointing first contact with the big screen as far as the entire *Star Trek* mythos is concerned.

CHAPTER SEVEN:

SAILING THE SILVER SCREEN (The Movie Trilogy)

In 1982, the second *Star Trek* feature, *Star Trek II: The Wrath of Khan* redressed the failing of its predecessor. It contains a strong, engaging plot, plenty of action, a powerful nemesis, dramatic relationships, a famous controversy— and a notorious continuity glitch.

Early in 1980, Leonard Nimoy, while promoting his television movie *Seizure: The Kathy Morris Story,* in which he played a neurosurgeon involved in a serious brain surgery case, had a few thoughts on *Star Trek* and its future, from this AP wire service report dated January 1, 1980:

Nimoy was just back from New York and Washington, where he had attended the premiere of Star Trek and promoted the movie on NBC's Today show.

Asked if he had signed yet for a Star Trek sequel, Nimoy, who starred in the television series of the same name, said, "There is nothing definite yet, but I gather there's a lot of conversation at Paramount about what to do with Star Trek next."

He said he does want to make something clear. "Some people have a conception that I have trouble playing other characters, that I'm too identified with Spock. It's no problem. It would probably be more dramatic to say it is.

"When I work in the theatre, I can feel it in the first few minutes on stage. Particularly from people who have seen me in Star Trek. They're trying to focus on Spock and what I'm going to be doing.

"When I played Sherlock Holmes, he was a character very close to Spock because of his logical deductions. But there was no problem."

But despite these protestations, Nimoy was really not too keen on reprising the role of Spock. A great deal of his reasons were derived from the fact that the shooting of *Star Trek: The Motion Picture* was a harried and unpleasant experience. The producers, he felt, had not used the characters or concepts well at all, and it was only with extreme reluctance that he approached a second *Star Trek* movie . Although he will not admit it today, Nimoy may have been the originator of the idea to kill off Spock in the second feature. At any rate, the idea did not give him much pause at all. Perhaps in shedding Spock for good, he might be able to pursue other career goals.

News of this leaked out early and caused great consternation among diehard *Star Trek* fans. Some of them went so far as to take out an ad in a major Hollywood trade paper predicting that Paramount would lose upwards of twenty million dollars, largely from a fan boycott, if they went through with what they considered murder. (Of a fictional character. . ?)

They were dead wrong.

For one thing, Paramount kept tight reigns on *Star Trek II*'s budget; it only cost thirteen million to make, less than a third of the maximum estimates of the first film's cost; on the other hand, it grossed eighty million in its initial domestic release alone. Paramount definitely made a bigtime profit on *Star Trek II: The Wrath of Khan.*

Hedging their bets over the Spock issue, the studio introduced a new (backup?) Vulcan character, Lieutenant Saavik, portrayed by Kirstie Alley. As director they hired Nicholas Meyer, a successful novelist (*The Seven Per Cent Solution*) turned movie director (*Time After Time* and the TV-movie *The Day After*), who brought a deft directorial hand and a humanizing touch to the proceedings. (His first film was a childhood effort, an 8-millimeter production of *Around The World In Eighty Days* financed by his father.) Altering the color scheme of the Enterprise sets and adding such sensible, human details as "no smoking" signs and fire extinguishers as well, Meyer was determined not to repeat the mistakes of the first movie. Still, he was a bit surprise to be involved at all:

Well, I never was anybody's first choice. I don't know how far down the line I was. I accepted it because I wanted to make Conjuring and they said, 'Make a big hit movie and you can do what you want.' Then I saw the first Star Trek film, they showed it to me, and I thought [that] i could make a better movie than this. That was good reason to do the sequel in that the first one had not fulfilled its promise. It had not been what it ought to be or what it could have been.

The thing that I cared about the TV series, and

what I thought made it special, was the people. To take them seriously, or more seriously than they'd ever been taken. The main subject of the film was aging and death. That's heavyweight stuff.

There was a lot of pressure to back off [from the downbeat ending]. They always [go] for the jugular when they want you to change things. They go for the one thing that makes it distinguished or distinctive. I said, let's be real, and everybody said, oh yes, let's be real. Then we got into how real real is. Then there was a flurry of back-pedaling about this and that, and you're going to kill the series. My interest was not in the series. My interest was in this movie, to make it the best because it has my name on it. and for me there was the task of making the people real.

These actors had played these parts to much and had, in a sense, got such a lock on them, such a fix. But what they were really fixed on, to some extent, was the television sensibility in which everything always ends up at the end of the hour back where it was at the beginning of the hour. The sensibility that I was trying to bring to it was completely separate. I said, "Big things are going to happen here, and everything is not going to be the same at the end as it was in the beginning." It's got everybody aging. That's antithetical to the notion of coming back to where you were. Aging and death. Kirk wears glasses. That was a kind of a shock (to them) at the beginning, but when they got to know me and trust me, then instead of being a liability, it became a challenge. Everybody got real excited. I think they breathed new life into those roles, they got so worked up about it. I loved them. I like the actors. I had a great time. It was fun to shoot with them.

One of the reasons I did this picture was to make the people real. That's all that interests me. Why can't Captain Kirk read a book? Why can't he do anything that we do? One of the things I had to back off on was having him smoke. There's a sign in the simulator saying "No Smoking On The Bridge." Somebody said they're not going to smoke in the 23rd Century. I said, "Why not?" They've been smoking for four hundred years. No one has given it up despite the Surgeon General's warning. Why can't they drink a cup of coffee? I keep thinking that the bridge was like the bridge of a destroyer with fog around and guys in pea jackets coming up with coffee. we decided they probably snorted Brim. But why can't Kirk read a book? And then the book I chose for him to read became loaded with significance.

Meyer was also intrigued to learn that the character of James T. Kirk had been based on that of Captain Horatio Hornblower.

That's what Shatner told me when I said that this was what I wanted to do, and he got very excited. That was the model for me: the adventures of Captain Hornblower. In fact, I made everyone watch the movie, the one with Gregory Peck directed by Raoul Walsh. The midshipman who was Scotty's nephew was stolen right out of that movie.

Special effects this time around were provided by Industrial Light and Magic, the effects company that grew out of George Lucas' *Star Wars* projects. Production began on November 9, 1981 and wrapped on January 2, 1982; after post production work was completed, the film was released on June 4, 1982. Meyer encountered some interesting problems during this period:

There were two kinds. There were the technical demands of working on the set, which is a difficult set to shoot. Most of the action takes place of that bridge, which is a three-hundred-and-sixty degree set, so that is lot of coverage you get rather bored with doing. The set is fiberglass, I think, so you can't staple any cards to it or anything. You have to tape things and tape is always coming down. It's hard to light there. There were technical problems, but every film presents some technical problems.

Making the film was very, very hard. One of the hardest things I ever did. I think one of the things that made it so much harder than it needed to be was that before we rolled the camera, Paramount had booked this movie into umpteen hundred theaters on June 4 [1982], which I didn't know. That didn't give much post-production time, the time used to complete the film. I can only contrast it with Time After Time. We finished shooting the movie Thanksgiving 1978 and the movie was released in October 1979, so I had, in effect, a year to finish the film. Five months to edit it. Editing is where films really get made. Dailies are like sentences in a book which hasn't been written yet. Editing is that process of trial and error, and also of contemplation. a five-month editing period is very useful for a movie. You can try things and change things and experiment and play around. I had a year to do it.

We finished shooting [The Wrath of Khan] February first and the film had to be shot during the day and edited at night and on special effects film. Normally, if this was George Lucas, we'd have a year to do that. But we had a month. I had two and a half weeks to edit the movie. When I discovered this was going to be the case, what happened was, in order to give myself a few more weeks, the film had to be shot during the day and edited at night and on weekends. That meant that for the period of six weeks plus, I had the curious experience of never seeing the light of day.

I would go to work at about five-thirty or six o'clock, before the sun had come up. I would eat lunch in a dark theatre looking at my dailies, so I'd never see the sunshine then. At night we would come out of the soundstages and I would go off to the editing room, by which time it was dark. On weekends I would also get up before sunrise and go down to the editing room. I wondered whether I would physically be able to stand it because I was putting in eighteen-hour days, seven days a week. That part of it was not fun. The shooting of it continued to be fun, but that was played against exhaustion.

I will never make a movie again in which I don't know beforehand that there is enough time to finish the film. We were such a photo-finish that we started printing the film— to make sixteen hundred prints takes three weeks in itself so count backwards from June fourth to May tenth or something like that— and then there were special effects coming in. ILM would send us down pieces of film with a label on it, shot 36A, and we would have to match that angle with shooting it. My cut of the movie when it was first put together was a fifty-percent "scene missing" or "insert missing."

Kirk would say "Fire," and then "scene missing." It made it very hard to tell about the movie.

Basically, changing the film is no big deal. Theoretically, you could keep changing right up until you print. But you will affect the sound. Sound effects are made up of many tracks. So if a reel of *film is a thousand feet long and somewhere four hundred and thirty-odd feet in, somebody knocks on the door, there's a separate reel of film that is black for four hundred and thirty-seven feet, there's a knock, and black for the rest of the reel. That is completely separate. Rayguns or whatever we're talking about are all on separate tracks. So you have as many as fifty or more separate soundtracks for the same reel of film. So what sound people keep hounding you for are what are called "locked reels," finished reels. My problem was that I was deprived of that period called contemplation, when you play with the film.*

If you suddenly have an epiphany, "Gee, I know now I can make it ten times better. Just remove thirteen frames from Spock opening his eyes so he opens them a little faster," or something at the beginning of the movie— that's hell to do that, and it costs a fortune.

The whole history is that this movie started out as nothing. This movie was to be made by the television department for a song and a prayer. They felt as though you've got these sets, they're all standing. . . they didn't realize that the sets had been completely vandalized; they had been completely ripped off. There was nothing. . . You've got all these sets, so let's get the actors and run them out in front and let the Star Trek money-making machine do its thing. They didn't really care about the movie, and that was reflected in the budget. They felt we could score it with a synthesizer, that would be all right. I said, why not a kazoo?

The process of making this film was that of turning the studio around and convincing them that we were going to do a class act and an event. Slowly, inch-by-inch, piccolo by violin, cello by trumpet, they retreated and gave ground. They said, "Why can't we do tracking?" [Tracking is] taking existing music from their library and laying it in some place else. I think the total effect is something like getting kissed over the telephone. we eventually changed their minds.

Now, I'm not a person who thinks you have to spend a lot of money necessarily to make something good, but you have to be able to afford what you are convinced you need. I was convinced that we needed a large orchestra for this.

On the other hand, I was not convinced that we needed to spend forty thousand for a composer, so we listened to a cassette. I met with James Horner and I really liked him a lot. He was real keen to do it. We were not real Star Trek fans when we started, but we became converted as time went on.

The film begins with most of the familiar Enterprise crew, plus the Vulcan Lieutenant Saavik (actually half Romulan, a point dropped from the movie), on the bridge of the ship. They Are responding to a distress call from the Kobayashi Maru, which is trapped in the Neutral Zone.

Klingons attack and incapacitate the ship; the order to abandon ship is given. The walls slide open and Admiral Kirk steps in; this has been a training simulation of a no-win situation, something all officers must be prepared to face. Later, Spock makes a cryptic reference to Kirk's unique approach to the Kobayashi Maru scenario when he was in Starfleet.

Spock gives Kirk a birthday present of a first edition of Dickens' *A Tale of Two Cities*. McCoy gives the Admiral a bottle of Romulan ale and a pair of glasses; Kirk is allergic to the sight-correcting medicines of the 23rd Century.

Meanwhile, Captain Clark Terrell of the U.S.S. Reliant is scouting a planet as a possible site for the mysterious Genesis project. Accompanying him is Commander Pavel Chekov. When they encounter cargo pods that have been converted into quarters, they become apprehensive, especially when Chekov sees something linking this spartan outpost with the Botany Bay.

Of course, Chekov was not yet assigned to the officer when the events of the first season *Star Trek* episode "Space Seed" occurred; although he would probably be aware of those events, this does not explain how the suddenly returning Khan Noonian Singh (Ricardo Montalban) recognizes Chekov as a former Enterprise officer. This is an unfortunate continuity glitch, but one which, if corrected, would have cost Chekov his big scene.

Khan, who has gone a bit over the edge in fifteen years of exile, then proceeds to introduce parasitic eels into the two men's brains in order to learn why they're there— and where to find James T. Kirk. Khan then takes over the Reliant and heads for Regula One, where the scientists Carol Marcus and her son David are working on the Genesis project.

Kirk gets wind that something is amiss at the Regula One station, and assumes command of his old ship, rounds up his old trusted companions, and heads out to investigate. The main officers learn that Genesis is a project that can transform a barren world to a flourishing garden, effectively creating life. Part of the problem, of course, is finding a completely barren world on which to test it.

The Reliant attacks the Enterprise before shields can be raised, causing extensive damage, and Khan reveals himself. Kirk volunteers to give himself up in exchange for the safety of his crew. Khan agrees as long as Kirk throws in everything concerning Genesis, and gives a sixty-second deadline for compliance. This gives Lieutenant Saavik time to access the codes to lower the Reliant's shields; the Enterprise strikes, and its wounded adversary withdraws.

At the Regula One station, Kirk finds devastation— and the unconscious forms of Chekov and Terrell, who, revived, explain Khan's actions. Kirk and McCoy beam down to the station's transporter's last coordinates, which take them inside a nearby asteroid; Kirk's last transmission to Spock is to head back to a Starbase in an hour, and comments on damage to the ship.

Dr. David Marcus and his mother Carol are there; David doesn't know that Kirk is his father. The two eel-infested officers then turn their weapons on Kirk and the others; they are still under Khan's control, and now are about to bring him the Genesis device. When he Orders the death of Kirk, however, Terrell resists, and turns his phaser on himself, vaporizing his body. The other eel then vacates the brain of Chekov, who falls to the ground.

It seems that they are all trapped inside the asteroid. Another no win situation. Saavik asks Kirk how he became the only person to beat the Kobayashi Maru scenario; he admits that he secretly reprogrammed the simulator. After the tension builds, Kirk then calls Spock on his communicator; their last exchange was a code designed to trick Khan into thinking the Enterprise was out of the picture.

With everyone safely transferred to the Enterprise, Kirk assumes command, and engages Khan in a game of cat-and-mouse in a nearby nebula cloud. In the course of the battle, everyone but Khan on the Reliant is killed.

Another exchange mortally wounds Khan, but he launches the Genesis device to the planet below before he expires. Kirk calls for Scotty to provide warp speed in three minutes. But Scotty has been knocked out and a key component has been shaken loose. Spock determines to enter the highly radioactive area to repair the damage; when McCoy bars his way, Spock nerve-pinches the doctor, places his hand against Bones' face, and whispers "remember." He then gives his own life in order to provide warp power; the Enterprise zooms away in the nick of time, just as the Genesis device explodes, transforming the planet.

A revived McCoy calls Kirk to engineering, where he witnesses the passing of Spock in a poignant final exchange of words.

A full funeral is given, and Spock's body is launched, in a photon torpedo casing, to the newly born Genesis planet below. It comes to rest in the lush jungle foliage of the newborn world.

Originally, Spock's death occurred midway through the movie, a placement altered by director Meyer:

I said he has to die at the end because there is no way you're going to top it. the movie is going to be anticlimactic if he dies in the middle, so I said he should die at the end.

With such an overwhelming climax, interest was immediately focused on the next picture. Was Spock *really* dead— and what part, if any, would Leonard Nimoy have in the production? He was certainly approached about it by the studio, although this information was kept under wraps until Paramount devised a means of linking Nimoy with *Star Trek III*— without revealing anything about the status of Spock.

During negotiations for *Star Trek III*, Leonard Nimoy rather offhandedly suggested that he thought he could direct as well as either of his predecessors, as he knew the basic material a bit more intimately than they did. To his surprise, producer Harve Bennett thought it was a good idea: and so a directorial career was launched, almost by accident.

Of course, from a marketing standpoint, it was a brilliant move. With Spock dead, *The Search For Spock* could be advertised using Leonard Nimoy's name— while at the same time preserving the mystery of the beloved Vulcan's ultimate fate. Nimoy's return was further brightened by a new enthusiasm for *Star Trek* brought about by a more positive experience on the previous film. The unpleasantness of the first feature was a matter of the past, as the cast had a great time under Nicholas Meyer's direction, and had finally regained the old camaraderie that was sadly missing from the first big-screen voyage.

Production on *Star Trek III* began on August 15, 1983 and principal photography was wrapped on October 21, 1983.

The Search For Spock begins begins with a black and white replay of Spock's final moments, which gradually fades into color. Kirk and the Enterprise are headed back to Earth, where Kirk is faced with the dreary prospect of a deskbound job.

Meanwhile, elsewhere in space, two Klingon ships are communicating. On one, Valkris, a female Klingon, is transmitting information to the captain of the other, Commander Kruge (Christopher Lloyd). This information concerns Kirk and the Genesis project. Once it is received, Kruge destroys the other vessel, making himself the sole bearer of this knowledge.

As the Enterprise enters spacedock, it passes the U.S.S. Excelsior, a new ship equipped with 'transwarp' drive. Meanwhile, sensors indicate a life form in Spock's sealed quarters; the door has been forced. A shadowed figure addresses Kirk when he enters, in Spock's voice, questioning Jim's decision to leave Spock on the Genesis planet. The figure turns out to Dr. McCoy, who utters a few more words on Spock's voice before collapsing. Everyone receives new assignments; Scotty is to be Captain of Engineering on the new Excelsior. The Enterprise is to be decommissioned. As for Kirk's desire to go back to Genesis, its a no-go situation, as Genesis has been quarantined.

Meanwhile, Kruge intends to investigate the vast power available on the Genesis world, which he hopes to use to further his own ambitions even as the Klingon Empire is negotiating for peace with the Federation.

Near Genesis, Dr. David Marcus and Lieutenant Saavik (now played by Robin Curtis) are scanning the planet from the U.S.S. Grissom (named for the pioneering astronaut who lost his life in the Apollo 11 disaster in 1967).

The Genesis device has provoked a bewildering variety of life and climate. Sensors also indicate a device exactly the size of Spock's coffin.

Kirk, Sulu, Chekov and Uhura are in Kirk's apartments, thinking of missing friends, when the doorbell rings. Kirk expects Scotty but is stunned to find Spock's father Sarek at the door instead. Sarek accuses Kirk of throwing away Spock's life; Kirk, he believes, was entrusted with Spock's soul, or *katra*. A mind meld reveals otherwise; the two men were separated by radiation shielding, and so the spark of Spock's essence was lost. Or so it seems. Kirk muses that Spock might have found a way to survive.

A search of the Enterprise records reveals the moment when Spock passed his spirit to McCoy. Sarek tells him that both McCoy and Spock must be taken to Mount Seleya on Vulcan so that both can be saved. Kirk swears to accomplish this seemingly impossible task.

On Genesis, Saavik and David find Spock's coffin— empty. A moan is heard in the distance as an earthquake strikes.

Kirk tries to sway Admiral Morrow into letting him take the Enterprise back to Genesis; Morrow refuses and suggests that Kirk had better reign in as he is threatening his career. Silently, Kirk resolves to go anyway.

Sulu and Chekov agree to help him.

McCoy, meanwhile, is trying to charter a vessel to take him to Genesis. A security officer overhearing this advises McCoy not to discuss that topic; McCoy attempts to use the Vulcan Nerve Pinch on the man. It doesn't work.

On Genesis, in the middle of a sudden snow storm, Saavik and David discover a naked Vulcan child. Apparently, the Genesis effect revived Spock's body in some fashion. The Captain of the Grissom, advised of this remarkable truth, attempts to contact Starfleet, but his ship is destroyed by Kruge's vessel, which suddenly decloaks.

Saavik draws out the confession that David had used a highly unstable substance to accelerate his Genesis research.

Kirk visits McCoy, who is about to be taken away for a long rest by the authorities. Kirk knocks out the security man and releases the doctor, who is less than pleased to learn that he's suffering from a Vulcan mind-meld. ("That green blooded son of a bitch— this is his revenge for all those arguments he lost!") It soon becomes readily apparent that all of Kirk's faithful officers are aiding him in his scheme to make off with the Enterprise.

As they head out of spacedock, the Excelsior is ordered to reclaim the enterprise and arrest Kirk. Convinced of his ship's superiority, he smugly calls for transwarp drive when the Enterprise goes into warp— but his engines fail, having been sabotaged by Scotty before the engineer "defected" to the service of Kirk.

Kruge lands on Genesis and fights off a microbe that has been evolved by the Genesis effect. Nearby, David reveals that the Genesis effect is going to break up the planet; both the world and Spock are aging in sudden leaps.

Kruge comes upon the hapless trio, but beams up to his ship when he hears word of the Enterprise's approach. Fortunately, Kirk surmises that a visual distortion in space probably indicates a cloaked vessel, and is ready when Kruge reveals himself, damaging the Klingon's ship.

The Enterprise suffers systems damage as well, but Kirk cannily covers up this fact, giving the Klingons two minutes to surrender. But Kruge reveals that he has prisoners and turns the tables by threatening to execute them. Saavik explains the situation in terse, oblique words. Kruge orders a prisoner killed; a Klingon prepares to stab Saavik in the back but David interferes and is killed instead.

Kirk, appalled at the death of his son, agrees to surrender but asks for a final minute with his crew. Kruge arrogantly grants him two minutes.

Kirk and crew engage the ship's autodestruct program; they then beam down to the planet just as Kruge's men beam over to the Enterprise bridge. One of Kruge's men informs Kruge that the ship is empty, with the computer speaking; Kruge listens in, and, apparently bilingual, realizes that it's a countdown, but its too late.

The Enterprise detonates, to be observed streaking across the sky like a comet by its crew on the planet's surface. Of the Klingons, only Kruge and Maltz (John Larroquette) remained on their Bird of Prey. The two Klingons on the planet are overpowered when Spock ages in another surge and throws one of them a great distance; Kirk nails the other one with his phaser.

Kruge beams down and gets the drop on the group; he has Maltz beam everyone but Kirk and the unconscious Spock to the Klingon vessel. The two commanders fight until Kirk wins; Kruge falls to his death after trying to do in Kirk who has graciously offered to save him.

Kirk then tricks Maltz into beaming him up and gets the drop on the last Klingon. Again, the crew (this time in a borrowed Klingon ship) escape from genesis as it explodes, this time in utter destruction.

Arriving at Vulcan, they are greeted by Uhura and Sarek. The Vulcan High Priestess, T'Lar, prepares to perform the necessary ritual.

It works, and Spock and McCoy are restored. Spock seems to have no memory of his friends, but his memory begins to come back when Kirk makes a deft turn on Spock's final words from *Star Trek II*. Spock then remembers Kirk's first name, and it becomes apparent that he is on his way to complete recovery.

Star Trek III's cost and profits were right in the same exact range as those of the third feature, so there was no doubt that there would be a fourth picture, and Leonard Nimoy was signed to direct once more, the first person to direct more than one film in the series.

An initial script draft was completed in August 1985 by the writing team of Steve Meerson and Peter Krikes. Another factor loomed as well: Paramount Picture's biggest box office draw, comedy superstar Eddie Murphy, appeared to be keenly interested in being in the film. Rumors abounded; many feared, and perhaps rightly, that Murphy would dominate the movie at the expense of the regular characters. Still, a role was written with him in mind, though it could have, in a pinch, been played by anyone.

Eventually, Murphy's attention turned elsewhere, and just as well, perhaps, as the combination of these two hot properties— Murphy and *Star Trek*— in one movie would not really have made as much money as two separate projects involving them on their own would have.

The script was later rewritten by producer Harve Bennett and Nicholas Meyer— the serious parts apparently by Bennett, and the humorous ones by Meyer. All four writers received screen credit after the Writer's Guild of America determined that all parties had contributed significantly to the project. Director Nimoy had some input as well, particularly in the choice of whales as the main focus of the plot.

The rough equivalent of the Eddie Murphy role became that of Dr. Gillian Taylor (Catherine Hicks), the focal Twentieth Century character. The movie also promised to feature the largest number of *Star Trek* alumni in any of the motion pictures; not only did Dr. Chapel, now a Commander (Majel Barrett) and Commander Janice Rand (Grace Lee Whitney) make their first appearances since *Star Trek: The Motion Picture*, but Sarek (Mark Lenard) and Amanda (Jane Wyatt) were on hand to check up on their son's well being.

The story of *The Voyage Home* begins a bit familiarly, as an alien probe travels through space beaming an indecipherable message. Meanwhile, debate is raging in the Federation Council in San Francisco, as tapes of the demise of the Enterprise are being observed, and a Klingon ambassador is denouncing Kirk as a criminal, backing up his arguments with a rather lopsided and distorted view of the events of *The Search For Spock*.

The Enterprise crew, meanwhile, is still on the planet Vulcan with their commandeered Klingon Bird of Prey, which Dr. McCoy has renamed the H.M.S. Bounty. Spock is being reeducated by computers and seems to be making great progress.

The alien probe, meanwhile, has rendered a number of starships defenseless, and has started to beam its signal at the oceans of Earth. The seas begin to boil and the sun is blotted out of the sky by atmospheric disturbances; Earth is helpless before this mysterious interloper.

Kirk and his companions, including Spock, head back to Earth to face the music, except for Saavik, who stays behind on Vulcan. When they near Earth, they find no one to greet them, as all communication has been overwhelmed by the strange probe.

They pick up a message from the Federation warning all vessels away from Earth. Spock listens to the strange message; after making adjustments to it considering that it's aimed at the oceans, he produces a somewhat different sound, which he soon identifies as the sound made by humpback whales— which have been extinct for three centuries.

After a brainstorming session, they decide to use the old whiplash-around-the-sun technique (it always worked on the TV show) in order to go back to the Twentieth Century and bring back a humpback whale, which they hope will be able to communicate with the alien device.

The attempt succeeds; the Warbird, cloaked, sets down in Golden Gate Park.

Chekov and Uhura search out some much needed uranium for the ship; Scotty, Bones and Sulu undertake the conversion of the cargo bay into an oversized aquarium; and Spock and Kirk try to find some whales. Having apparently grown weary of Twentieth-Century stocking caps, Spock (still dressed in Vulcan robes) ties a sash around his head to conceal his ears from prying eyes.

The search for whales leads them to a marine theme park, where Dr. Gillian Taylor is doing research with a pair of whales. Spock winds up swimming in the whale tank, mind melding with the cetaceans.

Needless to say, he and Kirk get chased away. But Spock has discovered that the whales are unhappy about the situation with humans, but that they will probably cooperate with Spock. Uhura and Chekov, meanwhile, have located uranium at a nearby naval facility— on the nuclear aircraft carrier, the U.S.S. Enterprise.

Dr. Gillian catches up with Kirk and Spock, quite by chance, and Kirk tries to pass off Spock's peculiarities by trying to pass him off as some sort of sixties burnout case ("I think he did too much LDS.") Spock alarms Gillian by mentioning that the female whale is pregnant, but she doesn't get any satisfactory answers from the strangers, only evasive answers that lead nowhere. Still, there's real chemistry between her and Kirk, and they wind up planning a date for dinner. (The man has moves, it seems, unlimited by temporal setting!)

Scotty and McCoy have no cash with which to buy the needed Plexiglass, so Scotty, after a brief consternation with primitive computing devices (he tries to talk to a desktop model using the mouse as a microphone, for instance) uses barter instead: at a plastics factory, he offers a scientist the formula for transparent aluminum in exchange for the needed materiel. This rouses McCoy's uncertainty, but Scotty just wonders if maybe the man didn't invent the stuff anyway, which assuages the doctor somewhat.

Meanwhile, over pizza and beer, Kirk hedges over his mission with Gillian. The whales are due to be transported to Alaskan waters, where it is hoped that they will survive. Kirk hints that he could take the whales somewhere where there safety would be guaranteed, but still holds back the more amazing aspects of his story. Finally, he springs the truth. Gillian does not believe him. Kirk is upset when he learns that the whales are being shipped out the very next day. Returning to the ship, he is extremely discouraged.

Meanwhile, Chekov and Uhura are draining power from the nuclear reactor of the aircraft carrier when the power drain is noted. Uhura contacts Scotty but the Klingon transporter is low on power; he beams her out but Chekov must wait, only to be captured by Marines. Interrogated by the FBI, he seems quite insane to his captors, especially when his phaser fails to function. He runs away, only to fall and be injured.

Gillian goes to the institute the next day to find that the whales have already been taken, ostensibly to avoid any media coverage. She becomes very upset and drives away to where she last saw Kirk. She arrives just in time to see Sulu lowering Plexiglass from a helicopter; it is guided into the invisible Klingon ship by Scotty, or rather by half of him, as his lower body is rendered invisible by the cloaking device.

Then, suddenly, she is beamed aboard by Kirk. Stunned, she has no choice but to accept his story now. But Chekov still remains to be rescued

from, as McCoy puts it rather scornfully, Twentieth Century medicine; he is on the verge of death in Mercy Hospital.

This action-laden sequence gives McCoy some amusing moments, as he is aghast at the hospital and would probably like to stay and help all of its patients from the primitive treatments they are about to undergo. Chekov is healed and absconded with; the mission can now get underway. Gillian gives Kirk the frequency of the whales' radio tracking transmitters, and he says goodbye to her— but she wraps her arms around him just as he is transported, winding up on the ship with him.

They fly to Alaska, only to find a whaling ship bearing down on the humpbacks. The whaler fires its harpoon, but it bounces harmlessly off the invisible hull of the cloaked spaceship. The Bird of Prey then decloaks and chases the whaler away. The whales are loaded, and the dangerous timesling effect is attempted once more. The Klingon ship returns to 23rd Century Earth at the same moment that it left, crashing into the ocean near the Golden Gate Bridge. The ship starts to sink, and the humans strive to escape; the hatch doors are jammed, trapping the whales, but Kirk swims down and blows the hatches. The whales swim free and soon begin to sing; the probe listens and stops its disruptions of the atmosphere, and soon departs Earth's solar system.

For their rescue of Earth, all charges against the former Enterprise crew are dropped except for the single charge against Admiral Kirk: he is found guilty of disobeying a direct order from a superior officer. As punishment he is demoted to Captain and given command of a new ship. Gillian heads off to join a science vessel; as an expert on whales, she already has a vital place in the 23rd Century, but she has a lot of catching up to do as well. But she and Kirk seem destined to meet again.

Finally, Kirk and his companions are ushered to their new assignment,which turns out to be the new, Constellation class Enterprise, NCC 1701-A.

But even as Kirk and crew prepared to take charge of their new vessel, yet another Enterprise was being launched. . with a baldheaded Frenchman as Captain, a woman doctor, an android science officer, and, horror of horrors, a *Klingon* on board! Many thought it couldn't, or perhaps even *shouldn't* happen, but Gene Roddenberry was going to give it one heck of a shot: a *Star Trek* series with an all new cast, set (somewhat vaguely) seventy-five or so years after the original series, and featuring the Enterprise of that farther future, the fifth of its line, NCC 1701-D. Paramount was banking that a syndicated show would generate them revenues, as well. It seemed impossible. But. . . it happened.

CHAPTER EIGHT:

A NEW GENERATION EMBARKS

For his new *Star Trek* series, Gene Roddenberry worked hard to produce a show that was true to the ideals of the first *Star Trek,* but one with its own flavor. As might be imagined, it took some doing; some of the characters took their time to settle in, but once they did, they were quite believable.

For starters, there was Captain Jean-Luc Picard. He was not to be the impetuous, dashing hothead Kirk, but rather an older, seasoned commander, well trained in the nuances of diplomatic relations, and with a long and distinguished career already behind him. His new command, the Enterprise NCC 1701-D, was the first of a new class of vessels. Its complement of over a thousand included entire families, as the lengthy space voyages it undertakes would otherwise keep families apart for years. It is, in essence, a world unto itself. But Picard, uncomfortable around children, is a bit dubious about this. Roddenberry had oceanographer Jacques Cousteau in mind when he created Picard.

For this demanding role, Roddenberry cast British actor Patrick Stewart, a noted Shakespearean who had roles in such films as *Excalibur, Life Force* and *Dune* in addition to his extensive stage work. Classically trained, he brings to the role of Picard much insight gained from portraying the kings and other great leaders of the classical drama.

Although basically cognizant of *Star Trek* and its characters, he was never aware, due to living in England, of the depth of the roots that the show has sunk deep into the American cultural mind. When he realized this, preparatory to joining the cast, he was a bit overwhelmed to realize that he would be trying to become a part of this remarkable phenomenon— a feat he has succeeded in amazingly well.

Patrick Stewart reveals that he was "compelled" to become an actor, "as a result of an argument."

At age 15, Stewart left school and landed a job on a local newspaper. He also happened to be an energetic amateur actor, which wasn't unusual since the English town of Mirfield (population 11,000) supported a dozen dramatic clubs. But the two vocations didn't mix.

"I was always faced with either covering an assignment or attending an important rehearsal or performance," he explains. "I used to get my colleagues to cover for me, but often I would just make up reports. Finally, I was found out. I had a terrific row with the editor who said, 'Either you decide to be a journalist, in which case you give up all of this acting nonsense, or you get off my paper.' I left his office, packed up my typewriter and walked out."

There followed two years of selling furniture. "I was better at selling furniture than I was at journalism," Stewart observes good naturedly. He also enrolled in drama school at the Bristol Old Vic to bring his skills up to the level of his enthusiasm.

The actor used to see his roles as a way of exploring other personalities and characteristics, but nowadays it has become more of a means of self-expression.

"When I was younger, I used to think in terms of how I could disguise myself in roles. Now I want my work to say something about me, contain more of my experience of the world.'

Patrick Stewart has become a highly regarded actor in Great Britain from his roles in such BBC productions as "I, Claudius," "Smiley's People," and "Tinker, Tailor, Soldier, Spy," all of which have aired in America.

His face is also known to American film-goers from roles in a variety of motion pictures. In the David Lynch adaptation of *Dune*, he played Gurney Halek, one of the more prominent roles in the film. In *Excalibur*, he played Leondegrance. More recently, he was seen in the strange science fiction film *Lifeforce* as the character Dr. Armstrong.

On stage, he starred in London in a production of "Who's Afraid of Virginia Woolf?" which garnered him the prestigious London Fringe Best Actor Award. As an associate artist of the Royal Shakespeare Company, Stewart is considered one of the leading talents of the British stage.

His impressive list of stage credits include Shylock, Henry IV, Leontes, King John, Titus Andronicus and many others. In 1986, he played the title role in Peter Shaffer's play "Yonadab" at the National Theater of Great Britain.

After Supervising Producer Robert Justman saw Stewart on stage at UCLA, the actor was cast as Captain Picard. "A friend of mine, an English professor, was lecturing and I was part of the stage presentation," he recalls. A few days later he was called to audition for *Star Trek: The Next Generation*. Since then, he has become a well-known face, although occasionally fans get confused. One woman accosted him at a party and racked her brains until she recognized him. "You fly the Endeavor," she told him triumphantly, when her memory finally clicked, "and you play William Shatner!"

One thing Picard would never do is beam down to an uncharted, possibly hostile planet. No vessel or force would risk its commander in such a foolhardy manner; Kirk was, in all frankness, often a reckless fool who, in real life, would have wound up dead as quick as those red-shirted one-time characters who served as phaser fodder on the old show.

Realizing this, Roddenberry in essence split the command function in two, providing Picard with an executive officer, William Riker. (In a nod to the old show's first pilot, as well as to nautical history in general, Riker is often referred to as "Number One.") Riker, a canny poker player among his other skills, is not afraid to take risks, but he weighs them carefully; one of his primary functions is to assure the safety of his superior officer.

The role of Riker was stepped into by Jonathan Frakes, a seasoned television actor.

"I knew this was a real part, a big one," says Jonathan Frakes regarding the six weeks of auditions he went through for the role, "and I had to get it."

The actor credits Gene Roddenberry with giving him the needed insight into the character that eventually became his.

"Gene is so very non-Hollywood and really quite paternal. One of the things he said to me was, 'You have a Machiavellian glint in your eye. Life is a bowl of cherries.' I think Gene feels that way, which is why he writes the way he does. He's very positive and Commander Riker will reflect that," states Frakes.

The actor sees Riker, the executive officer and second in command of the Enterprise as, "strong, centered, honorable and somewhat driven. His job is to provide Captain Picard with the most efficiently run ship and the best prepared crew he can. Because of this he seems to maintain a more military bearing than the other characters in behavior, despite the fact that salutes and other military protocol no longer exist in the 24th Century."

While Frakes cannot help but regard this role as "a real step up in my career," he's had recurring roles on other series such as *Falcon Crest, Paper Dolls* and *Bare Essence*. For a year he was even a regular on the daytime drama *The Doctors*.

Other television appearances include a role in the made-for-TV movie *The Nutcracker* and critically praised roles in the mini-series *Dream West* and both parts of the extended mini-series *North & South*. The actor has also appeared both on and off-Broadway and in regional theatre productions.

Born and raised in Pennsylvania, Frakes did undergraduate work at Penn State before going to Harvard. He also spent several seasons with the Loeb Drama Center and then moved to New York.

"I gave myself a five year limit," he reveals. "If I wasn't making a living at acting in five years, I would find something else to do. After a year and a half of being the worst waiter in New York and screwing up my back as a furniture mover I got a role in 'Shenandoah' on Broadway and then landed a part in *The Doctors*." Then his career was off and running.

Frakes spent the next five years in New York City and then moved to Los Angeles in 1979, at the suggestion of his agent. There he landed work immediately in episodic television.

"I really have been very lucky. There's a cliché in this business that says, the easy part of being an actor is doing the job. The hardest part is getting the job."

Jonathan Frakes resides in Los Angeles and is married to actress Genie Davis, who appears on *The Days of Our Lives*.

Roddenberry also created a new function for *The Next Generation,* that of Ship's Counsellor, and a new alien race, the Betazoids, to go along with it. Although this position can be occupied by a member of any race, Picard is highly fortunate in that his ship's counsellor is a Betazoid.

Betazoids are an extremely empathic, if not telepathic, race who can read other's minds to varying degrees; Picard's counsellor, Deanna Troi, is a gorgeous woman, half-human, who can sense emotions with great acuity. Combined with extensive psychological training, this makes her input a vital part of the Captain's decision making process— and makes "Captain, I sense. . ." as familiar a line to *Next Generation* fans as "I'm a doctor, not a. . ." was for "Bones" McCoy.

Deanna once had a relationship with Riker, but now they seem to have mellowed into an abiding friendship.

A British actress, Marina Sirtis had been working in various roles in England for years before she decided to give the colonies a try, but she landed the continuing role of Deanna Troi after being in America only six months. "It's taken me years to become an overnight success," she quips. "I had a six-month visa, which was quickly running out. In fact, I got the call telling me I had the part only hours before I was to leave for the airport to return home."

Marina enjoys the irony of being a British actress playing an alien on American television. But viewers won't notice a British accent coming out of an alien being as she's devised a combination of accents for the character to use.

"In the 24th Century, geographical or nationalistic barriers are not so evident. The Earth as a planet is your country, your nationality. I didn't want anyone to be able to pin down my accent to any particular country, and being good at accents, the producers trusted me to come up with something appropriate, Sirtis states.

Counsellor Troi is like an empath in that she can open her mind to the feelings and sensations of those around her, unlike a full Betazoid telepath.

Sirtis initially auditioned for the role of Security Chief Tasha Yar, rather than that of Deanna Troi.

"After my third audition for Tasha, I was literally walking out the door when they called me back to read for Deanna. While I was looking at the script, director Corey Allen came in and said, 'You have something personally that the character should have. . . an empathy, so use it.' I love being able to play someone who is so deep with that kind of insight into people, particularly since I usually get cast as the hard 1980s stereotype."

Born to Greek parents in North London, Marina demonstrated an inclination towards performing at an early age. "My mother tells me that when I was three, I used to stand up on the seat of the bus and sing to the other passengers." But her parents wanted their daughter to follow "more serious" pursuits. So after finishing high school, Marina had to secretly apply to the Guild Hall School of Music and Drama, where she was accepted. "My first job after graduating was as Ophelia in 'Hamlet' for the Worthing Repertory Company."

Following that, she worked for a few years in British television, musical theatre and in other repertory companies throughout England and Europe. She landed some supporting roles in features such as *The Wicked Lady* with Faye Dunaway and in *Deathwish III* opposite Charles Bronson.

She decided to stay on in the United States and has settled in Los Angeles where she watches "far too much MTV" and keeps track of her local soccer team in London, in which she owns a few shares. Her brother is a professional soccer player.

Marina has always been interested in the stars and space exploration and believes that she once saw a UFO. "I was working with a repertory company in Worthing, a seaside town in England. One night as I was walking down the street, I saw this huge orange thing in the sky. At first I thought it must be the moon, but it was very off color. It was very close, but too high to be a balloon. Apparently a lot of other people saw it, too."

Most controversial at the show's inception was the android science officer Data, whom many saw as a transparent Spock substitute. Indeed, one can find many similarities between the two, but the differences are what have been developed most.

Whereas Spock has emotions which are subdued but still lie latent beneath his stoical surface, Data, quite literally, has none. (On the other hand, he often serves as *The Next Generation's*

prime dispenser of plot-smoothing sciencespeak.) But intrigued by humans, Data strives, as a complete outsider, to understand them, and hopes to cultivate emotions of his own.

Although he is always conscious of his lack of feelings and his inability to love, there is often an irony surrounding this character, as his actions, shaped by his strivings, generally display all of the highest human qualities, even though he is generally unaware of this.

The late Philip K. Dick, a science fiction writer intensely concerned with what makes humans authentically human, would probably have considered Data the most human character in *The Next Generation*. In fact, it's a shame he passed away in 1982, as he would probably have written a great Data story.

As Data, Roddenberry cast the Texas-born Brent Spiner. "I'm one of those people who believes that mankind will find all the answers out in space," says Spiner, "but the first step is to get off this planet. The sun is going to burn out eventually and we better be somewhere else as a race of people by the time that happens. I think that's why everybody digs Star Trek. They know its a part of all of our futures and represents a vision of home."

The character played by Spiner is not human, but he is not an alien. Data is an android who can pass for human and even graduated from Starfleet Academy with top honors.

"As the series opens we don't know much about Data, only that he was constructed by beings on a planet which no longer exists. He's the only thing left. His creators programmed him with a world of knowledge— he's virtually an encyclopedia— but only in terms of information, not behavior. He's totally innocent. However, he does possess a sense of question and wonder that allows him to evolve. His objective is to be as human as possible."

Brent Spiner was born and raised in Houston where he saw an average of three movies a day between the ages of 11 and 15.

"At fifteen I was already a major film buff. I could quote lines from movies, tell you who was in it and in what year it was made. I always fantasized about being an actor. I was also lucky enough to have a brilliant teacher in high school named Cecil Pickett, who was capable of seeing potential, nurturing it and making me aware of it."

Spiner did a lot of "gritty, ugly plays" off-Broadway after college. "The one that finally pushed me over into the serious actor category was a public theatre production of 'The Seagull' for Joseph Papp." The actor went on to roles in the Broadway musical productions of 'Sunday In The Park With George,' 'The Three Musketeers,' and 'Big River,' based on Mark Twain's *Huckleberry Finn*.

Since moving to Los Angeles in 1984, he's appeared in such plays as 'Little Shop of Horrors' at the Westwood Playhouse. His feature film credits include the Woody Allen film *Stardust Memories*. On television he has appeared on such series as *The Twilight Zone, Hill Street Blues, Cheers* and *Night Court*.

One could say that he was very well prepared for his role as Data by his belief in extraterrestrials. "Obviously I'm from another planet," he laughs, but adds that he seriously does believe in beings from other planets and will continue to do so until such things are disproven.

An Enterprise without a ship's doctor, of course, would have been unthinkable, and so Roddenberry provided one in the person of Chief Medical Officer Beverly Crusher. A compassionate, dedicated doctor, she is also the mother of a precocious youngster, Wesley Crusher.

Her late husband, Jack Crusher, was killed while under Jean-Luc Picard's command; it was Picard who broke the news to the bereaved family. But after some initial discomfort, Beverly Crusher has had no problems working with Picard— and there has been some indication that her feelings for him may run deeper than mere friendship.

Dr. Crusher is the first regular role in a television series for actress Gates McFadden. Her character is presented with more background than most of the others as she is the mother of Wesley Crusher, and the widow of the man who died while saving Picard's life on an earlier mission.

Gates trained to be a dancer when quite young, while growing up in Cuyahoga Falls, Ohio. "I had extraordinary teachers: one was primarily a ballerina and the other had been in a circus. I grew up thinking most ballerinas knew how to ride the unicycle, tap dance and do handsprings. Consequently, I was an oddball to other dancers."

Her interest in acting was sparked by community theatre and a touring Shakespeare company. "When I was ten, my brother and I attended back-to-back Shakespeare for eight days in a musty, nearly empty theatre. There were twelve actors who played all the parts. I couldn't get over it— the same people in costumes every day, but playing new characters. It was like visiting somewhere but never wanting to leave."

She earned her Bachelor of Arts in Theatre from Brandeis University while continuing to study acting, dance and mime. Just prior to graduation she met Jack LeCoq and credits the experience with changing her life.

"I attended his first workshop in the United States. His theatrical vision and the breadth of its scope were astonishing. I left for Paris as soon as possible to continue to study acting with LeCoq at his school. We worked constantly in juxtapositions.

One explored immobility in order to better understand movement. One explored silence in order to better understand sound and language. It was theatrical research involving many mediums. Just living in a foreign country where you have to speak and think in another language cracks your head open. It was both terrifying and freeing. Suddenly I was taking more risks in my acting."

McFadden lives in New York City where she has been involved in film and theatre both as an actress and director-choreographer. Her acting credits include leads in the New York productions of Michael Brady's "To Gillian On Her 37th Birthday," Mary Gallagher's "How To Say Goodbye," Caryl Churchill's "Cloud 9" and, in California, in the La Jolla Playhouse production of "The Matchmaker" with Linda Hunt.

Gates was the director of choreography and puppet movement for the late Jim Henson's *Labyrinth* and assisted Gavin Milar in the staging of the fantasy sequences for *Dreamchild*. "Those films were my baptism by fire into the world of special effects and computerized props," Gates reveals.

Another character (eventually to be promoted to the post of Chief Engineer) devised for the new show was Geordi LaForge, named after the late *Star Trek* fan George LaForge, a cerebral palsy sufferer whose long survival was attributed to his strong identification with the show. A black man, Geordi maintains the tradition of a multi-ethnic cast in *Star Trek,* and is also blind; but, due to the advanced technology of the 24th Century, he can see by means of an electronic visor linked with his nervous system. He can even see into visual ranges inaccessible by most human beings.

Geordi is a sincere, likeable, confident character; he has some slight insecurities, but he always perseveres, and makes a point to communicate freely with others. Almost the opposite of Picard, he affects an informal approach to life, and is not hung up on protocol.

The portrayal of Geordi LaForge was undertaken by actor LeVar Burton, best known as the young Kunta Kinte on the classic mini-series *Roots,* based on Alex Hailey's novel of the same name. Before becoming an actor, Burton wanted to become a priest— and even entered a seminary at the early age of thirteen.

By the age of fifteen, however, he had discovered the world of philosophy, and gave up his sacrosanct ambitions. The closest thing to being a priest, he reasoned, was now becoming an actor, a goal he pursued with great vigor; he received superlative reviews for his work in *Roots,* and has long been the host of PBS' *Reading Rainbow,* a series aimed at promoting literacy among children. But it was *Roots* that launched his career.

It was during his sophomore year at USC, while only 19, that he auditioned and landed the pivotal role of the young Kunta Kinte.

"I think the producers had exhausted all the normal means of finding professional talent and were beating the bushes at the drama schools," the actor ventures. The role would win him an Emmy nomination and subsequent acting roles, which prevented his return to college.

Burton starred in a number of made-for-TV movies such as the Emmy-nominated *Dummy, One In A Million: The Ron LeFlore Story, Grambling's White Tiger, The Guyana Tragedy: The Story Of Jim Jones, Battered, Billy: Portrait of a Street Kid,* and the mini-series *Liberty.* The actor has also been the host of PBS' highly acclaimed children's series *Reading Rainbow* since its inception in 1983. Among his film credits are *Looking For Mr. Goodbar, The Hunter* (with Steve McQueen) and *The Supernaturals* (with Nichelle Nichols).

The actor was born in Landsthul, West Germany, where his father was a photographer in the Signal Corps, Third Armored Division. His mother was first and educator, then for years a social worker who is currently working in administration for the County of Sacramento Department of Mental Health. Burton is single and resides in Los Angeles with his German Shepherd, Mozart.

Tasha Yar, the security chief on the new Enterprise, is not as at ease as Geordi; having survived a brutal society on her home planet, she has channelled all her energies into self control, but there is also a warm person striving to express herself through her self-imposed discipline.

Tasha Yar was portrayed by Denise Crosby, the granddaughter of famed crooner Bing Crosby.

Denise Crosby described the character she played with this thumbnail sketch. "She comes from an incredibly violent and aggressive Earth colony where life was a constant battle for survival. She can fight and she knows her job, but she has no family, is emotionally insecure and somehow feels that she doesn't quite belong on this ship of seemingly perfect people."

As the granddaughter of the late legendary crooner Bing Crosby, Denise enjoyed the part and even related to it to some extent.

"My grandfather was a Hollywood legend. Growing up with that wasn't exactly normal or typical either, and I think that helps me understand Tasha's imbalance and insecurities," explained the actress in a first season interview.

Prior to getting involved in developing an acting career, Denise went through what she describes as her "European runway model thing. I hated modeling, but I was taken to Europe by three California designers who were trying to launch their fashions there. I loved London, so I just stayed on."

When she returned home for the Christmas holidays, she was almost tapped for an acting role.

"Toni Howard was casting a movie called *Diary of a Teenage Hitchhiker* and had seen my picture in a magazine. I looked wild. My hair was about a quarter of an inch all the way around. I wore army fatigues and no makeup." While she didn't land that role, Toni Howard encouraged her to enroll in acting classes. The roles soon followed.

Her feature film credits include *48 Hours, Arizona Heat, The Eliminators, The Man Who Loved Women, Trail of the Pink Panther* and *Miracle Mile.*

The TV credits for Denise also include *L.A. Law, Days of Our Lives, The Flash,* and the made-for-TV movies *O'Hara, Stark, Malice In Wonderland* and *Cocaine: One Man's Poison.*

Denise has also appeared in some local Los Angeles theatre productions, including the critically well-received "Tamara", in which she had the lead, as well as the controversial one-act play "Stops Along The Way" directed by Richard Dreyfuss.

But the biggest shocker in *The Next Generation's* crew roster was Worf. . . a Klingon. It seems that in the years since Kirk's heyday, a peace treaty has finally been negotiated between the Federation and the Klingon Empire. (Some may recall that some negotiations were underway at the time of the events of *Star Trek III: The Search For Spock,* a fact referred to by Commander Kruge in that film.)

The two spheres of influence strive to get along, and have established some basis for mutual trust. There are not, however, any other Klingons in Star Fleet; Worf is a unique case, having been raised by humans after his family was killed in the massacre of their outpost during a surprise Klingon attack. . . an event that will come back to haunt Worf again and again.

In this manner, he is even more like Spock than Data is. He is the product of two cultures, a warrior Klingon dedicated to his own culture but tempered by exposure to human ideals. Worf was added after the pilot for *The Next Generation* and so does not appear in "Encounter At Farpoint." For a while, he would be little more than a grouchy guy with lots of hair standing in the background recommending aggressive action. However, he would soon be featured in more and more episodes which would eventually open up a window on the fascinating world of the Klingon people. This was no more than a matter of speculation in the days of Kirk.

Cast as Worf was the 6' 5" actor Michael Dorn. As a longtime *Star Trek* fan, Dorn says that this role "was a dream come true. First, because I'm a Trekkie and second, I'm playing a Klingon, a character so totally different from the nice-guy roles I'd done in the past. Worf is the only Klingon aboard the Enterprise. That still makes him an outsider which is okay by me because Worf knows he's superior to these weak humans. But he never lets the other crew members see that because he's a soldier first and second."

The actor gives enthusiastic praise to series creator Gene Roddenberry for having the "genius and vision" to depict an optimistic future in which a peaceful alliance could be struck between Earth and the Klingon Empire. "Gene believes there is good in everybody— even Klingons!"

Dorn enjoys playing very different kinds of characters, and knows what its like to appear in a series after playing a regular on *CHIPS* for three years. "I love doing cop roles, and as a highway patrolman I got to drive fast and I never got hurt."

Dorn hails from Liling, Texas, but he was raised in Pasadena, California, just minutes away from Hollywood. He performed in a rock band during high school and college and in 1973 moved away to San Francisco where he worked at a variety of jobs.

When he returned to L.A., he continued playing in rock bands until a friend's father, an assistant director of *The Mary Tyler Moore Show,* suggested the young man try his hand at acting. Dorn can be seen in the background, as a newswriter, in episodes from that classic comedy's last two seasons.

"I had done a little modelling by this time and had studied drama and TV producing in college. Once I started, I caught the bug."

His first acting role was a guest spot on the series *WEB,* a show based on the satirical film *Network.* Dorn was introduced to an agent by the producer of the show and began studying with Charles Conrad. Six months later Dorn was cast in *CHIPS.* Following that series, Dorn resumed acting classes. "I worked very hard; the jobs started coming and the roles got meatier."

Dorn has made guest appearances on nearly every major series, most notably *Hotel*, *Knots Landing* and *Falcon Crest*. He has also had recurring roles on *Days Of Our Lives* and *Capitol*. His feature film credits include *Demon Seed*, *Rocky* and *The Jagged Edge*.

Dorn hopes eventually to direct, but for now, "I want to take one step at a time and do the best work I can do." He's still interested in rock music, plays in a band, does studio work as a bass player and writes music in his spare time.

With the cast finally set, *The Next Generation* got under way at last. Gene Roddenberry handed the executive producer's reins over to Paramount's Rick Berman. D.C. Fontana signed on as story editor, but soon left, unhappy with such things as the treatment received by her script "Encounter At Farpoint."

As "Encounter At Farpoint" begins, Captain Picard has just been posted to the new Enterprise (NCC 1701-D). He doesn't even have a first officer yet, but is taking the ship to Farpoint Station to pick him up.

Suddenly, Deanna Troi, an empath, senses a powerful mind scanning them and ahead they detect a strange grid in space. A being appears who calls himself "Q". He states, "You are notified that your kind has infiltrated the galaxy too far already. You are directed to return to your own solar system immediately."

When a crewman draws his phaser in an attempt to subdue Q, the being freezes the crewman solid. Picard points out that the weapons had been set on stun, to which Q responds that he would not want to be captured in a helpless state by humans.

Q demonstrates his knowledge of human history, but Picard points out that everything Q has described is centuries out of date. Humans are far different now, and Picard doesn't fear the facts. This gives Q an idea and he departs to make preparations. As soon as he leaves, Picard orders the Enterprise to maximum warp. He and other bridge crew members descend to the battle bridge so that a saucer separation can take place, which sends the part of the ship with families off in another direction.

As expected, Q catches up with them and Picard surrenders to be taken before Q for judgement. Picard, Tasha, Troi and Data are taken to what appears to be a trial chamber from the preholocaust period. They fence with words and Q impetuously freezes Troi and Tasha, but finally unfreezes them when Data plays back Q's assurance that the prisoners would not be harmed. Finally Q decides to submit the Enterprise crew to a test and chooses their destination of Farpoint station as the perfect examination of their merits. Q returns the four to the Enterprise.

On Farpoint, Riker is meeting with the Administrator Zorn, and has a curious encounter when he mentions that he wishes he had an apple and suddenly finds a bowl full on the counter when he could have sworn they weren't there a moment before. When Riker leaves the office, Zorn seems to be speaking to empty air when he threatens to punish someone if they ever do anything like that again.

Riker encounters Dr. Crusher and her son Wesley, who are also awaiting the arrival of the Enterprise. They have a similar experience when she is looking for a certain style of cloth which appears where a moment before a different style had been hanging.

While walking around, Riker encounters Geordi and Markham, who have also been posted to the Enterprise.

The stardrive section of the Enterprise arrives in orbit around Farpoint. Riker is beamed aboard to meet Picard. There he is briefed on what has just happened. The saucer section arrives about an hour later and Riker oversees the rejoining.

Elsewhere on the Enterprise, Data is escorting an admiral to the shuttle bay because he refuses to use the transporter. It is Dr. McCoy, now 147, who has been overseeing the medical lay-out. He is impressed with the new Enterprise and tells Data, "You treat her like a lady. She'll always bring you home.'

Picard meets with Dr. Crusher and expresses concern that she might not have wanted to be posted there. She states otherwise. Picard thought she might harbor a grudge because her husband died while under Picard's command.

Later, Picard is sending a farewell message to Admiral McCoy when Q appears on the bridge and states that they are taking too long and have only 24 hours to solve the mystery of Farpoint. Q vanishes; Picard states that he will not act any more quickly that usual. He won't be rushed into making a rash decision.

Picard, Riker and Troi beam down and go to Zorn's office. There Troi reveals that she is detecting great pain, loneliness and terrible despair. Zorn is offended by this, particularly when Picard doesn't believe Zorn when he states that he has no idea what Troi could be encountering, or why.

Wesley talks his mother into letting him accompany her to the bridge, where he peers out from the turbolift. At first Picard is annoyed to see him, but when he learns that the boy is Dr. Crusher's son he allows him to come on to the bridge.

Down at Farpoint, Riker, Data, Troi, Tasha and Geordi do some exploring to try to learn what's going on. They find underground passageways and Troi feels that she is very close to the source of the pain.

Just then, an unknown spacecraft approaches the planet and begins firing on it. The blast hits the Bandi city but not Farpoint station itself. The ground team beams back to the Enterprise. Then Q reappears, mocking Picard and his efforts, coaxing him to blast the intruding ship.

Riker and Data have stayed behind and make their way to Zorn's office. He pleads for help but insists he doesn't know what's happening, or why. Suddenly he vanishes before their eyes in a transport beam. He has been taken aboard the other vessel.

Picard guesses what must have happened and he orders Farpoint evacuated and then an energy beam sent down to the planet.

Farpoint was actually a gigantic alien being which had been wounded and landed on the planet. The Bandi captured it and enslaved its transformation powers, but now its mate has found it. Energized by the Enterprise, the enslaved being can now free itself, and it leaves with the other creature, which frees Zorn.

Q is disappointed that the humans passed the test and didn't use brute force against what they didn't understand, but the being promises that there will be other times and other places. Picard orders Q off his ship, stating that the only one proven guilty of savagery here is Q himself.

Sadly, "Encounter at Farpoint" kicked off the new series with something less than a bang. The initial story, by D.C. Fontana, had Gene Roddenberry's "Q" plot slapped onto it; the two plots don't even cross over, much less merge. Instead of a genuine, two-hour movie, audiences received a poorly-shuffled sandwich of two separate stories. . . with no meat in between.

Like *Star Trek: The Motion Picture*, "Encounter At Farpoint" was slow moving and all too enamored of its own special effects, which featured a saucer/hull separation as a climactic moment. Special effects for this and other first season episodes were provided by Industrial Light And Magic, but they soon proved too expensive, and other effects teams were sought out. With a per-episode budget of over a million dollars, *The Next Generation* was a major gamble for Paramount, and they had to use that budget to the best of their ability.

"The Naked Now" was a virtual remake of "The Naked Time." It reveals a few things about the characters, but not much, beyond demonstrating just how annoying Wesley could be. "Code of Honor" continued this distressing string of similarities to the old show.

"The Last Outpost" introduced the Ferengi, the new villains, who don't make much of an impression in their initial foray.

"Where No One Has Gone Before," reflecting the new show's lack of gender bias, used Wesley fairly well and introduced the Traveller, an alien who, after a fashion, becomes one with his own mathematical equations and casts the ship into distant unexplored regions of space.

"Lonely Among Us" had an alien stowaway on the Enterprise making trouble; not for the last time, either.

"Justice" condemned Wesley to death for violating a seemingly trivial taboo on a planet of blonde fitness fiends.

"The Battle" provided information on how Picard lost his old ship the Stargazer in a battle with Ferengi; the old nemesis he defeated then shows up with revenge on his mind.

"Hide and Q" brought back Q, and much too soon. Here, he offers Riker powers which tempt the first officer to play god.

"Haven" introduced Deanna Troi's vexing mother Lwaxana, played by Majel Barrett. (Wonder how she got the job. . .) A muddled plot involving an arranged marriage and a plague ship echoes memories of "For The World Is Hollow And I Have Touched the Sky."

"The Big Goodbye" introduced Captain Picard's passion for hardboiled detective fiction, as well as the holodeck concept. While Picard is off playing Dixon Hill. private eye in a simulated 1940s San Francisco, a malfunction causes the characters in the program to develop real personalities. . .and real bullets in their guns.

"Datalore" is an evil twin story enlivened by Bret Spiner's dual role of nice and not-so-nice androids. It clears up some of the mystery of Data's origin, but not much else. It does demonstrate that Spiner is an actor to watch.

"Angel One" threatens the crew with a deadly plague, but everything works out in the end.

"11001001" found the all-but-empty Enterprise being stolen by aliens while Riker and Picard are distracted by a charming woman, Minuet, in a holodeck fantasy. The imaginary Minuet makes quite an impression on Riker, but there's no chance of anything ever really happening between them.

"Too Short A Season" took an Admiral Jameson back to a planet where he resolved a crisis in his youth. The new crisis was really a ruse set up to lure the now-aged Jameson into the vengeful clutches of an old nemesis, but the Admiral had ill-advisedly taken a huge dose of an alien anti-aging drug and arrived at his destination in the full vigor of youth. Complications ensue, as his use of the drug violates his prescription.

In "When The Bough Breaks," sterile aliens kidnap seven children— including Wesley— to renew their race. It doesn't work. "Home Soil" and "Coming of Age" are adequate episodes. Things pick up with "Heart of Glory," the first episode to focus on Worf as more than just a grouchy guy who's handy with a phaser. Renegade Klingons fleeing from the Empire try to involve Worf in their rebellion, provoking a serious conflict of interest for him.

After the action-heavy "Arsenal of Freedom," the show suddenly gets relevant in "Symbiosis," in which the medicine one planet provides to keep another from dying of an ancient plague is revealed to actually be a highly addictive drug. "Skin of Evil" kills off Tasha Yar rather offhandedly, then gives her a nice funeral.

In "We'll Always Have Paris," the husband of an old flame of Picard's accidentally triggers time distortions which only Data can cope with; Picard recreates, on the holodeck, the date where he stood the woman up years earlier.

"Conspiracy" reveals that the Federation has been infiltrated by evil bugs from a distant, but Picard gets to the bottom of it and finally gets to use a phaser on someone in the series.

The first season wound up with "The Neutral Zone," a strangely inconclusive episode involving 20th Century Terrans who experience future shock after being revived from cryonic suspension. The Romulans reappear, probably since the Ferengi were a washout as heavies, but the show's ending is weak and inconclusive, and the season just sort of fizzled out.

SEASON TWO

The second season of *The Next Generation* showed a marked improvement over its first. A number of changes were evident. First, Jonathan Frakes now sported a beard; some viewers, unimpressed by the first season, now use the sight of a clean-shaven Riker as their cue not to watch an episode, while a hirsute Frakes indicates a better than average chance of a good episode.

Claiming that Gates McFadden's character just didn't click with the rest of the cast, Roddenberry summarily dropped Beverly Crusher from the roster with an offhand mention of her going off to head Starfleet Medical. Her replacement was another woman, Doctor Pulaski, ably played by Diana Muldaur, a veteran guest star of the original *Star Trek*. Despite Muldaur's fine acting, however, this character definitely did not click at all.

Perhaps the problem was that the crusty, no-nonsense Pulaski was, in many respects, a female "Bones" McCoy. The character provided some much-needed friction on the bridge, but for some reason this never really came to bear on the plots much, leaving her a somewhat distant and un-engaging character.

Another new character also came on board, although she may have been there all along; Guinan, a mysterious alien woman of great age who functions as bartender and freelance counsellor in the Enterprise's open lounge, Ten Forward, serving synthahol, a marvelous brew whose mildly intoxicating effects can be shaken off at will.

The role of Guinan was created for Whoopi Goldberg, who loved the show as a child and was inspired by its message of racial harmony, as exemplified by Nichelle Nichols. Goldberg actually sought out a role on the show; she might even have been on the first season if the The Next Generation's producers hadn't that that her friend LeVar Burton's reference to her interest in the show wasn't serious.

Guinan's background is shrouded intentionally, with tantalizing bits occasionally thrown out that only serve to deepen the mystery. It is known that Guinan's people were scattered when their home world was destroyed by the Borg; it also comes to light that she has had dealings with Q—who is actually somewhat afraid of her. The real strength of the character lies in her great sympathy for all other living creatures— perhaps the reason for her chosen occupation of bartender. Although not featured on a weekly basis, Guinan is a recurring presence in The Next Generation.

Whoopi Goldberg described her character Guinan as "a cross between Yoda and William F. Buckley," but freely admits that she's put a lot of herself into the role as well. Growing up in New York, young Whoopi was inspired by the harmonious message of the original Star Trek, and especially by Nichelle Nichols.

When Goldberg learned that her friend LeVar Burton would be on a new Star Trek series, she asked him to tell Gene Roddenberry that she wanted to be on the program, too—but the producers of The Next Generation thought he was joking. A year later, Goldberg took matters into her own hands and contacted Gene Roddenberry; the two worked together to create the mysterious alien bartender who runs Ten Forward, a popular gathering place for the crew of the Enterprise.

Although Whoopi's first showbiz experience took place at the age of eight, there was a large gap in her career, as she raised a child and, at one time, contended with a heroin problem. She worked at a variety of jobs, including one in a funeral parlor whose owner had a curious sense of humor, and 'initiated' his employees by hiding in a body bin and playing "zombie," scaring them witless in the process. Whoopi was not amused.

By the time the 1980's rolled around, she was active in theatre and comedy, working in Southern California with the San Diego Repertory Theatre and putting on a number of one-woman shows. (She also washed dishes at the Big Kitchen restaurant, where the menu still carries a special named after her.) In 1985 she got her big break, in Steven Spielberg's film of The Color Purple, in a role which earned her an Oscar nomination and the Golden Globe Award. Since then she has starred in Jumpin' Jack Flash, Burglar, Fatal Beauty, Clara's Heart and Homer and Eddie.

Her role as psychic Oda Mae in Ghost netted her the Oscar for Best Supporting Actress, and she continues to work in such films as The Long Walk Home (with Sissy Spacek) and Soapdish.

She has also won an Emmy for her 1986 guest appearance on Moonlighting, and starred in the CBS sitcom Bagdad Cafe with Jean Stapleton.

She is concerned with the plight of our nation's homeless, and has, with Robin Williams and Billy Crystal, been a prime force behind the annual Comic Relief benefit concerts. In 1989, her various charity projects resulted in her being granted the Starlight Foundation's Humanitarian of the Year.

Still active on stage, Goldberg has performed in Moms, The Spook Show, and Living On The Edge of Chaos, as well as returning to the San Diego Repertory Theatre, a.k.a. The Rep, to take part in fund raising performances (along with Patrick Stewart) for that organization.

The second season's opening episode was delayed until November by the Writer's Guild strike, and that first entry was in fact based on a script submitted to the once-planned *Star Trek* revival series which was supplanted by the first movie. Rewritten for the new cast of characters, "The Child" is conceived upon Deanna Troi by an alien entity which wants to learn about humans by becoming one.

The resultant offspring grows at a rapid rate, but must abandon its physical body when it realizes that it is the source of the deadly radiation affecting the safety of its newfound family. A touching if manipulative story, this one gave Marina Sirtis plenty of emotion to work with.

"Where Silence Has Lease" loses the Enterprise in a vast void provided by a malevolently curious being; curious about death, it plans to examine all the possible ways humans can die. This process should require no more than two thirds of Picard's crew, but this does not deter the captain from fighting back with his wits.

In "Elementary, Dear Data," Geordi is annoyed by Data's Holodeck Sherlock Holmes simulation, as the android has captured the logic but not the mystery of the stories. So, Geordi programs in an adversary worthy of— in a crucial slip of the tongue— Data, which makes Moriarity a match for the android. The professor, now "real," begins to learn about the Enterprise, and eventually kidnaps Dr. Pulaski in a ploy to be granted life outside the holodeck.

"The Outrageous Okona" veered into idiocy as Data tried to learn about humor from a 20th Century standup comic created by the holodeck. Joe Piscopo guest starred. The other plot was also weak, focusing on a Romeo-and-Juliet type affair involving a pair of vapid interstellar teens.

"Loud As A Whisper" featured a real deaf-mute actor, Howie Seago, as a similarly affected negotiator who communicates through three telepathic companions; when they are destroyed in a senseless misunderstanding, he abandons his mission of peace until Deanna can give him hope again.

"The Schizoid Man" was in fact Data, his personality impinged upon by a brilliant but dying scientist who sees the android as his ticket to immortality. The arrogant scientist cannot carry off the masquerade in silence and is soon revealed; getting him to relinquish his second chance at life is another matter entirely, but when he realizes

the harm he's done he returns control to Data and gives up the ghost, as it were.

"Unnatural Selection" not only subjects Dr. Pulaski to an aging disease like the one in "The Deadly Years," it solves the problem using the transporter matrix— the same solution used in a similar episode of the animated *Star Trek* series. The only real suspense comes from the difficulty in finding a transporter trace for Pulaski, as she avoids using the device at all costs. Diana Muldaur does a fine job in the only episode that does her character any justice at all.

Now that the Federation and the Klingon Empire are friends, it seems inevitable that an officer exchange program should be initiated; in "A Matter of Honor," Riker gets first shot at it and jumps at the chance. Here he must learn to eat Klingon food, fend off the advances of Klingon women, and betray his captain. . . this last as a matter of duty, of course. a fascinating look at the Klingons, imbedded in a genuinely suspenseful plot.

As this episode begins, Mendoc, a Benzite ensign, joins the Enterprise crew as part of an ongoing officer exchange program. When Picard mentions an opening on the Klingon ship Pagh, Riker volunteers to be the first human to serve with the Klingons. Worf helps him learn about Klingon customs: the First Officer's primary obligation, on a Klingon ship, is to kill his captain if the captain seems weak or indecisive. The Second Officer is likewise obligated to his immediate superior. Riker also prepares by sampling Klingon food in Ten Forward, much to the disgust of Pulaski and other humans.

As Riker is about to beam over to the Pagh, Worf gives him an emergency transponder. While the two ships rendezvous, Mendoc notes a patch of microbiotic organisms on the hull of the Pagh, but says nothing: Benzite procedure requires a complete analysis before making a report.

The Klingons question their new human officer, and Riker swears loyalty to the captain and the ship. When his Second Officer challenges his authority, he beats him soundly, thus winning his respect. Captain K'Arganis greatly amused by this.

The Enterprise discovers the microbe— a subatomic bacteria that eats metal— on its hull, and the Benzite mentions that he'd noticed it on the

Klingon ship too. The Enterprise determines that the microbe has eaten a 12 centimeter hole in the Pagh's hull by this point, and follows the Klingon ship to warn it.

Riker impresses the Klingons by eating their food, but stalls when he learns that one dish he'd eaten cooked on the Enterprise is actually eaten alive by Klingons. The two Klingon women aboard express curiosity about Riker, prompting some ribald humor— Riker realizes that they have a sense of humor, even if it isn't very sophisticated, and joins in their laughter. They even discuss Klingon family matters.

One Klingon is proud of his father's heroic death, while the other is ashamed that his father was once captured by Romulans, escaped, and now awaits a quiet, natural death on their homeworld.

When Riker returns to the bridge, the Captain has discovered the hole in the hull, and believes that the Enterprise is responsible. The fact that a scan beam (courtesy of Mendoc) was focused on the area for several minutes only fuels his suspicion, which he turns on Riker.

Riker stands his ground; having vowed loyalty, he will serve the Pagh even in an attack on the Enterprise. When the Captain demands the Enterprise's security codes and other secrets, however, Riker refuses, since it would violate other oaths he has made. The Captain says that he would have killed Riker on the spot, as a traitor, if he had revealed those secrets; now he may have the honor of dying in battle among Klingons.

Meanwhile, the Enterprise has found a means of removing the microbes, and sends a message out to the Klingons. K'Argan does not believe them, and prepares to attack. The Enterprise, unaware of this, cannot locate the cloaked vessel. K'Argan prepares to fire, and also gives this honor to Riker. Riker says he will obey, but tells the captain that his reasons are wrong, and triggers the transponder. K'Argan demands the device, which Riker yields to him.

The Enterprise locates the transponder beacon, and beams Riker aboard— only to find an angry Klingon captain aboard the bridge instead. Worf subdues K'Argan and puts him under guard. Riker hails the Enterprise, as acting Captain of the Pagh, and demands the surrender of the Federa-

tion ship. Picard surrenders, and the Klingons decloak, ready to be rid of the microbe. K'Argan returns to his ship.

Riker has cleverly maintained the honor of all involved. His only shortcoming, in Klingon eyes, was that he did not assassinate his superior officer. K'Argan strikes Riker a vicious blow, which Riker does not duck, thus reestablishing K'Argan's authority. Riker returns to the Enterprise, after what may have been the shortest exchange assignment on record.

"The Measure of a Man" is essentially a courtroom drama in which an ambitious science officer, intent on disassembling Data to see how he works, questions the android's rights as a sentient being, provoking Picard to mount an eloquent defense (with a little help from Guinan).

"The Dauphin" is a young woman being transported to her home world where she can, hopefully, affect the course of a long-standing feud, to which she represents the key. She becomes friends with Wesley, but their romance is hindered by the young lady's shapeshifting chaperone— and the fact that the girl is in fact also a shapeshifter.

"Contagion" in this case is digital, as the U.S.S. Yamato is destroyed by a computer program from an alien probe. The same fate threatens the Enterprise, as well as a Romulan ship intent on interfering. Data's apparent death provides the key to solving this problem, and Picard is forced to destroy a fascinating alien teleportation device for security reasons.

"The Royale" traps an Away Team in a strange casino, which turns out to be an illusion created by aliens for the benefit of an injured astronaut. Long after his death, the illusion continues, and Riker and his team cannot get out until they fulfill the plot requirements of the 20th Century potboiler novel on which the casino's reality is based.

"The Icarus Factor" pits Riker against his competitive and annoying father. The subplot, in which Worf's friends recreate an important Klingon ritual on the holodeck, is far more interesting.

"Pen Pals" puts Data into contact with an alien child with a primitive radio set. When her planet is revealed to be torn by immense seismic disturbances, Data wants to rescue her, but Picard refuses to let him, invoking the Prime Directive. Nevertheless, the allegedly inhuman android is intent upon helping his unseen friend.

Q is a more serious threat than usual in "Q Who," as he hurls the Enterprise far into uncharted space— and introduces them to the Borg. Guinan and Q are revealed to have met centuries earlier; it is not a cheerful reunion. This episode probably reveals more about Guinan than any other, but as usual, any answers about her only serve to raise more questions.

"Up The Long Ladder" involves a race of clones who try to obtain genetic material from the Enterprise crew in order to revitalize their race. Basically, after numerous generations they're producing shoddy copies of the original settlers. When they steal cells from Riker and some others things really heat up. Fortunately, an answer to their problem lies right around the corner in an adjacent subplot involving a cargo hold full of displaced rural colonists, inexplicably Irish in accent, who agree to move to the clones' world, if only the clones can get used to the idea of reproducing by what can only be termed the old fashioned way.

"The Emissary" is K'Ehleyr, a half-human Klingon woman, who embarks on a tumultuous romance with Worf while trying to help the Enterprise rendezvous with a shipload of Klingons about to revive from cryonic suspension. Arriving too late, Picard is faced with a group of Klingons who still think there's a war on. Worf and K'Ehleyr pull off a masterful ruse: the Klingons could never accept that the Federation won the war, so they trick them into believing that the Empire was triumphant. Worf assumes command of the Enterprise for this brief but crucial period; deception is an accepted and honored Klingon method of facing a challenge.

In "Peak Performance," Riker must refurbish and command an abandoned frigate in war games against Picard and the Enterprise, a part of Federation preparedness against a potential Borg threat. With both ships rigged with simulated weapons systems, they are sitting ducks for a Ferengi captain who cannot believe that there is nothing of value hidden somewhere in this pe-

culiar situation. Riker and crew must somehow work their way out of this predicament; fortunately, they were preparing to cheat in the war games, and have an ace up their collective sleeve.

The season fizzles out with a bargain-basement episode, "Shades of Gray." Riker, infected with a deadly virus, dreams scenes from past episodes. How convenient. Pulaski saves him, of course, in her last stand as attending physician on the Enterprise.

This is a weak, if not downright pathetic, conclusion to a season which improved immeasurably of the first season. Almost any other episode— "Q Who," "The Emissary" or "A Matter of Honor"— would have seen the season out with a bang rather than a whimper.

Still, the show had more than overcome the founderings of its first season, and had proven that it could stand on its own. The next season would be even better.

CHAPTER NINE:

THE OLD GUARD STUMBLES; THE NEW WAVE TRIUMPHS

While *Star Trek: The Next Generation* continued to pick up steam and to gain recognition, things did not work out quite so well for the classic *Star Trek* characters. *Star Trek V: The Final Frontier,* directed by William Shatner, was a distinct disappointment to film-goers— and to Paramount Pictures as well.

Part of the problem was the use the characters were put to. Shatner's attempts at humor and character development revealed an unhappy truth: Leonard Nimoy may have known how to utilize the characters he'd been familiar with for over twenty years— but Shatner hadn't learned half as much

Using Scotty to get an extremely cheap laugh by having him bang his head on a bulkhead after stating how extensive his knowledge of the new Enterprise is was a far cry from the character-based humor of *The Voyage Home.*

And although it is possible for someone to foster hidden feelings for a close associate for years, having Scotty proclaim his attraction to Uhura after two decades of silence produces nothing more than an awkward moment for audiences and cast alike. Shatner's meddling in the script did nothing to smooth its progress; by adding a newfound half-brother for Spock, he effectively cut Spock's screen strength in half, and, not coincidentally, strengthening the focus on Kirk as the main character.

Not all the fault lay with Shatner. Paramount, convinced that humor was *the* key to the success of a Star Trek movie (after all, *The Voyage Home* was funny, *and* it made 110 million dollars), insisted on having comedic moments even if they seemed to come out of nowhere.

A promotional tag, asking why theaters were putting seatbelts in the theaters that summer (Shatner actually stated that the studio had really considered this ploy!), was intended by Paramount to suggest the excitement *Star Trek V* had to offer, but the question was neatly answered, and most unflatteringly, by a *Starlog* writer: "To keep the audience from leaving!"

One well-known television movie critic had this to say: "If *Star Trek: The Final Frontier* is indeed the final big-screen effort, it's a rather dismal way to end it all. This *Star Trek* seems to be a futile reach into the past rather than a dynamic soaring into the future." (Dixie Watley, *At The Movies*)

Strictly from a box-office standpoint, this feature was a washout. Costing thirty-two million dollars to make, it grossed only fifty million dollars, less than half the take of *The Voyage Home*.

Shatner landed the role of director by pressuring Paramount to give him a shot at it. He'd already received the green light by the time *Star Trek IV* was to be released; the supporting actors were unhappy to note that Shatner was almost hoping that Nimoy's second film would take a nosedive.

Not only would this make him the potential saviour of the series, but it would give him a chance to cut costs— by dropping everyone but Captain Kirk and Mr. Spock from the script. This scheme was mercifully erased when *Star Trek IV* broke all *Trek* box office records.

Quick to allay suspicion, Shatner told *Starlog*:

The story centers around Kirk, Spock and McCoy, but I've carefully choreographed special moments for everybody into this film. Nobody was ignored. What I've attempted to do in Star Trek V is to establish relationships between characters that haven't been there before. Scotty and Uhura, for example, are doing something a little bit different this time around. But I've taken great pains to have each character do something he or she hasn't done before.

Unfortunately, those "things" revealed just how limited Shatner's understanding of those characters was.

Nimoy, meanwhile, was enjoying great success as the director of the smash hit *Three Men And A Baby*. When Shatner's negotiations with Paramount Pictures proved sluggish, Nimoy took another job, directing *The Good Mother* for Touchstone Pictures. (The film, starring Diane Keaton, was not a great success but received perhaps the best critical notices of Nimoy's efforts to date.) This led to another delay in the startup of *Star Trek V*'s production, prompting the petulant Shatner to threaten to do a Spockless feature; but

when Nimoy called his bluff, he was forced to admit that he couldn't do it without Nimoy. Production was also stymied by 1988's writer's strike by the Screen Writer's Guild, which endured well into the fall of that year.

Even when Nimoy came on board, as it were, things were not destined to run too smoothly. Nimoy didn't think much of Shatner's story idea, which involved Spock's heretofore unknown brother popping up out of nowhere and commandeering the Enterprise. Nimoy even went so far as to tell Shatner that if they filmed the script (outlined by Shatner and scripted by Harve Bennett and David Loughery) as written, they would be laughed off the screen!

Apparently, Shatner's tension in the role of first-time movie director was immense; he'd only directed a few episodes of his TV vehicle *T.J. Hooker* before this, and perhaps feared that he was in over his head. Shatner's apprehension was perhaps best described by Leonard Nimoy on a *Tonight Show* appearance promoting the film's June 1989 release:

"I gave him one piece of advice the first couple of days of shooting. I said, 'Stop talking so fast.' It's the sign of a first-time director. You come on a stage the first day on the set and you're excited and you've got the adrenaline going and you're nervous and if you want to spot a first-time director, you look for the guy with the sweaty palms and he's hyperventilating and he's talking too fast. He thought that by talking fast it would speed up the schedule, but you couldn't understand a word he was saying."

According to extras on the set, Shatner was so worked up on the set at one point that he actually knocked off his own toupee. A furious Shatner immediately sacked all the extras for that day's work, as they could not refrain from laughing at this humorous spectacle. On a more humble note, Shatner did, at one point, admit that he needed all the help he could get, and welcomed advice.

Of the film's budget, much can be said about its size. Six million apiece to Shatner and Nimoy (for acting only) trimmed the thirty-two million dollar budget down to twenty. After the director's salary and the rest of the cast's renumerations, things were pretty slim, and Paramount decided to eschew the use of George

Lucas' Industrial Light and Magic's services. Ultimately, the effects for the film's climax were not as effective as they could or should have been.

The final word, ultimately, was in the box-office receipts.

(When *Star Trek V* was released on home video, it was ticketed at $89.95, as opposed to the more reasonable $29.95 price of the previous three features— a blatant effort to get home video buyers to help make up for the deficit on Shatner's directorial debut.)

Still, Shatner was undeterred by his maiden effort's lackluster showing, and has since announced plans to direct a sequel to the Z-grade horror picture *Kingdom of the Spiders*, in which Shatner starred in the 1970s.

 Close on the heels of this debacle came the season premiere of *Star Trek: The Next Generation*. Getting off to an adequate start, it would prove to be *The Next Generation's* best season yet. Repenting of his dismissal of Gates McFadden— the character of Dr. Pulaski never caught on, and fans wrote in requesting McFadden's return— Roddenberry brought back Beverly Crusher as the Enterprise's Chief Medical Officer. No mention was made of her tenure as head of Starfleet Medical (presumably a rotating position?), and Pulaski was not even referred to; her whereabouts were left unknown. (A treatment devised by Pulaski was referred to in a later episode, however.)

Early in the season, executive producer Rick Berman hired writer Michael Piller, who soon achieved the rank of executive producer himself. His task was to oversee scripts for the show.

Piller was responsible largely for the great increase in script quality; in fact, he seemed to specialize in finding ways to create engaging stories in spite of Gene Roddenberry's rather stringent format guidelines, which forbade, among other things, even the slightest hint of conflict between members of the Enterprise crew. Piller's arrival was a crucial factor in the show's ever-growing vitality.

Also on hand was a new model of the Enterprise, a four-foot model which generally supplanted the six- and two-foot models built at the series' in-ception. This was the work of Dan Curry and Robert Legato, the show's special effects wizards. Supplanting Industrial Light and Magic early in the first season, they developed new and more flexible ways to present the Enterprise using digital visual compositing rather than optical film effects; this approach makes it possible to add a theoretically limitless number of elements to a shot without any loss of image clarity.

As the series proceeds, they build a library of shots which can be altered and reused without any risk of redundancy; the library would eventually contain hundreds of shots. As for the new model, it was easier to use that the six-footer, which was, however, the only model with hull separation capacity. The six-footer was also a very complex piece of lighting wiring; the new model simplified things considerably with a flexible neon system. (The windows and interior lights are actually visual effects composited on later in the shooting process.)

With these changes in place, the third season revved up with "Evolution," involving one of Wesley's science projects gone awry, as microscopic nanites begin to eat the computer core of the Enterprise. A scientist preparing to observe a rare stellar event is perturbed by this interference and tries to kill the by-now sentient creatures, provoking their displeasure. But with Data as an interface, communications are established and things are ironed out.

In "Ensigns of Command," Data is assigned to get a human colony off a planet before the aliens with legal rights to that world arrive and destroy them. Unfortunately, they are determined to stand and fight, and the android officer must use less that tactful means to convince them of just how overwhelming an enemy they are faced with.

Picard, meanwhile, tries to stall the aliens by finding a loophole in their agreement with the Federation, which unfortunately happens to be one of the longest, most exacting documents in human history. Meanwhile, Data makes a more-than-scientific impression on a young woman cyberneticist, and learns something about kissing.

"The Survivors," a human man and his wife, occupy a small patch of green on a planet otherwise utterly destroyed by an alien attack. They have no desire to be rescued. An alien ship drives the Enterprise off but something in its behavior triggers Picard's suspicions, and he returns.

The ship seems to be trying to keep the Enterprise away from the survivors. It turns out that the man is a powerful alien who fell in love on Earth years before and maintained human form when he married. When his wife died in the attack he was so grief stricken that he used his powers to destroy the aliens— not just the attacking force but the entire race! Guilt ridden by this genocide, he has exiled himself to this world, creating an illusion of his wife, as well as the ship to protect his privacy. Picard wisely leaves him alone to endure his self-imposed exile from the rest of the universe.

"Who's Watching The Watchers" casts Picard as an unwilling god when a Federation observation post on a developing world is discovered by the inhabitants. A native, injured in an accident, is beamed up to the Enterprise for medical treatment but wakes up long enough to see the captain.

When he returns to his world he brings word of this new god. This causes complications for Riker and Deanna as they search, disguised as the Vulcan-like locals, for a missing member of the observation team. Picard finally beams down to explain that he's only human, but his would-be disciple refuses to take even this at face value. An intriguing episode.

"The Bonding" is another key Worf episode. When a member of an Away Team commanded by the surly Klingon is killed, the guilt ridden Worf feels responsibility for the woman's orphaned son. So does an alien entity on the planet , which tries to assuage the boy's loss by recreating his dead mother. Fortunately, the being is convinced that this would not be in the boy's long term interests, and the story ends as Worf and the boy undergo a Klingon brotherhood ritual. A good episode despite the alien's motivational similarity to that of the alien in "The Survivor."

In "Booby Trap," Geordi recreates the woman who designed the Enterprise's warp drive on the holodeck in order to work up a solution to the fact that the ship is trapped by an ancient energy-draining device. This idea works out— but Geordi falls for the illusion of Leah Brahms.

"The Enemy" finds Geordi stranded on a hostile planet where he must overcome a wounded Romulan's suspicions and gain his trust in order for them both to survive. Another Romulan is taken aboard the Enterprise, where a blood transfusion is needed to save his life, but the only compatible donor, Worf, refuses to help, as his parents were killed by Romulans.

"The Price" details negotiations for a potentially valuable wormhole; the Ferengi, now played as completely greed-addled buffoons, crash the negotiations and effectively knock the Federation's negotiator out of the picture by provoking an allergic reaction.

Riker's poker playing skills lead Picard to make him the replacement negotiator, but the real danger at the table is a secret Betazoid misusing his powers to gain an edge as well as to romance Deanna Troi. However, he misjudges her ethically, and closes the deal before the wormhole is determined to be unstable.

"The Vengeance Factor" involves Picard in establishing diplomatic relations between a planet and a pirate-like band that split away a generation earlier. While transporting the planet's leader, Riker becomes involved with her assistant, who is actually carrying a genetically engineered poison in her system that is fatal to members of a specific clan. He realizes this in time to save the negotiations but is forced to kill her to prevent another murder. He is left shaken.

"The Defector" is a Romulan admiral determined to prevent a sneak attack by his Empire. Naturally, Picard doubts his story, and it turns out to be a Romulan ploy to capture a Federation ship. But the admiral was sincere, having been used by his own government.

Picard escapes the Neutral Zone trap by revealing a pair of wild cards up his sleeve: he's been accompanied by two cloaked Klingon ships all along. The admiral commits suicide, leaving a heartfelt letter that can never be delivered to his family until the two sides achieve a lasting peace.

"The Hunted" examines the nature of soldiers in peacetime. A planet transformed some of its citizens into perfect soldiers and shipped them off to a sequestered colony once the war was won;

the soldiers want their normal lives restored. The Enterprise stumbles into the midst of this when they help capture an escaped "prisoner" who is one of these soldiers. In a fitting conclusion, the soldiers and the government are caught in a standoff. Picard invokes the Prime Directive and clears out, leaving this particular society to work out its problems on its own.

"The High Ground" involves Picard and Beverly Crusher in a terrorist/ hostage situation; the terrorists have legitimate grievances but go too far, as does the oppressive government in combating resistance. An intriguing story that loses force by trying to straddle both sides of a difficult and emotionally charged issue, "The High Ground" is essentially the situation in Northern Ireland watered down to the point of inanity and cast in a science fictional form.

Q shows up, stripped of his powers by his peers, in "Deja Q." Picard takes some convincing that Q is not responsible for his current crisis, which involves a moon with a decaying orbit.

Q learns humility of sorts when an old nemesis of his shows up and threatens the Enterprise; he leads it away in a shuttlecraft, and is awarded with the restoration of his powers for this selfless act.

Needless to say, his humility dries up pretty quick, but he does save the planet threatened by its moon, forces Picard to listen to mariachi music, and enables Data to enjoy a good laugh.

"A Matter of Perspective" is basically *Rashomon* in space, as the holodeck is used to recreate the varying accounts of a situation in which Riker may have committed murder. Of course, he is cleared of all charges.

"Yesterday's Enterprise" introduces a temporal distortion which casts the Enterprise into an alternative history where the Federation is losing a long running war with the Klingons. Since this prevented the crew from meeting the creature in "Skin of Evil," Tasha Yar is back on board, in place of Worf, who's missing for obvious reasons.

Guinan alone senses that something is wrong, and struggles to convince Picard that reality can be changed. The earlier Enterprise which has caused the time shift must ultimately go back

through the time rift and face its fate. It will be destroyed defending a Klingon outpost from a surprise Romulan attack, thus making peace between the Klingons and the Federation. Tasha, sensing that her death in the other timeline was meaningless, joins the other ship, and normality is restored, with no one but Guinan the wiser.

"The Offspring" is Lal, an android 'daughter' created by Data. This is a very touching episode. Suspense is introduced by having the Federation attempt to take her away for study, as in "The Measure of a Man," as if the legal precedent set there had no weight.

Picard is willing to risk his career to protect the androids' rights, but the issue becomes moot when Lal malfunctions and dies, after having developed the emotions her 'father' lacks. This marks the directorial debut of Jonathan Frakes, who handles the sensitive emotions of this tale with great aplomb.

In "The Sins of the Father, " the Enterprise crew is in for a rough ride when a Klingon exchange officer temporarily assumes Riker's duties. The over-worked crew can't help but notice that Worf is the only one escaping the Klingon's discipline; what they fail to realize is that being polite and condescending to a fellow Klingon is a very pointed way of insulting him.

Worf at last cannot stand it any longer, and is ready to fight the visitor, only to learn that the Klingon is actually his younger brother, and that his insults were a test. Now that Worf has shown his worthiness, his brother reveals his secret: when Worf and his parents went to the outpost later destroyed by the Romulans, the younger brother was left behind, presumed dead by the Empire but actually raised by another family.

He has sought out Worf after all these years because their father has now been accused of helping the Romulan's notorious attack, and only the eldest son can challenge charges of treachery in the High Council. Otherwise, the stigma of a traitor will be borne by their family for seven generations. One further catch: if Worf's challenge fails he will be executed.

Picard has Data access all the records of the massacre. The charges against Worf's father were based on the records of a recently captured Romulan vessel. Data compares these to the sensor records of the Federation ship Intrepid, which was nearby at the time, and discovers a discrepancy in the time codes. Someone has tampered with the Romulan records.

Picard and Riker accompany Worf and his brother to the Klingon home world. Worf's brother is ambushed but survives. Picard steps in as Worf's "second." The Council sessions seem to offer little hope for Worf's cause until Data also learns that another Klingon— Worf's nurse— survived the massacre as well.

Picard ventures into the heart of the ancient Klingon capitol to find her, only to have her refuse his aid. On his way back he is attacked by assassins and nearly loses his life. He is saved only by the old woman's change of heart, for she stabs the assassin in the back.

Her appearance at the Council throws things into an uproar. The head of the Council calls everyone into his private chambers. The truth is revealed: the father of Worf's accuser was the real traitor. When the Romulan records were seized, this information threatened the entire power structure of the Empire, for the traitor was a member of a very ancient and powerful family.

Since Worf, apparently the sole survivor of his line, was away serving in Starfleet, a decision was made to cast the blame on his father. No one believed that he would ever challenge the charges. According to Klingon ideals, the honor of the Empire outweighs that of any single family, a point that even Worf must agree upon.

It seems that he and his brother must die, until he proposes another alternative. He agrees to undergo discommendation, in effect "de-Klingonizing" himself, accepting the blight on his family name and exiling himself from the Empire.

Although this is humiliating, it shows true Klingon honor, for it demonstrates loyalty to the Empire and also leaves open the margin, however slight, of someday gaining revenge.

In "Allegiance," Picard is replaced by a double and himself imprisoned with three other aliens (one of whom is actually one of their captors in disguise). While Picard must try to generate cooperation between his new companions, the Enterprise crew must contend with the peculiarities of the impostor. Fortunately, Riker takes

command just in time to divert a major disaster.

"Captain's Holiday" leads Picard into trouble and romance, thanks to Riker's mischievous suggestion intended to make the vacation a bit more interesting. Time travellers, Ferengi and the beautiful if unethical archaeologist Vash provide the staid captain with a week he won't forget, although he doesn't get much reading done as per his original plan.

"Tin Man" is the name given an alien artifact, apparently a sentient spacecraft. Tam, a Betazoid born with full powers is assigned to make contact. His telepathy, untempered by slow development, makes it hard for him to avoid the constant mental chatter of most beings, but he becomes friends of sorts with Data, whose mind is closed to him.

When a Romulan craft approached 'Tin Man," Tam alerts it, revealing the full extent of his mental reach, and it lashes out, destroying the intruder. Ultimately, Tam joins with the spaceship, which was awaiting death by supernova after the death of its crew, and they disappear into the universe after sweeping the Enterprise and a second Romulan ship away from the range of the exploding star.

"Hollow Pursuits" introduces the potentially sticky subject of holodeck abuse, as Barclay, one of Geordi's engineering team, uses the deck to vent his frustrations and explore his fantasies, using his superior officers as characters in his creations. Unfortunately, Barclay's work is suffering, even though he may be very capable of helping solve the Enterprise's latest problem— which he does, once his own problem is discovered and addressed.

A good performance by Dwight Schultz enlivens this intriguing episode; apparently, Barclay is too much the innocent to have used the holodeck in any *seriously* twisted way, even though he obviously has a thing for Deanna.

In "The Most Toys" Data is kidnaped (and his destruction faked) by an avaricious collector. Although intrigued at being filed alongside a Roger Maris baseball card (complete with recreated bubblegum odor), Data will not comply with his captor's wishes until a woman is threatened.

The woman tries to help Data escape and dies for

her troubles. Data is finally located and beamed away just as he is about to shoot the villain with a disrupter, having concluded that the man will only inflict more pain and death if he is not destroyed. This is an intriguing lesson for android, who supposedly could not kill in earlier episodes but here admits to being able to use lethal force. Obviously, difficult moral decisions are also within his powers.

Spock's father "Sarek" appears in this episode which bears his name, but his vital diplomatic mission is threatened by an encroaching form of senility, rare among Vulcans but overwhelming when it strikes. It induces the Vulcan's strong emotions, long suppressed, to break out, causing turmoil among the crew.

Sarek finds it hard to face the truth, but when he does, a Vulcan mind meld with Picard enables him to finish his task in top form, while Picard valiantly copes with Sarek's set-aside emotions— which include anguish at his relationship with his famous son. This episode also reveals that a young Lieutenant Jean-Luc Picard was actually in attendance at Spock's wedding years earlier.

In "Menage a Trois," Deanna is captured, along with Riker and her mother, by a Ferengi who finds Lwaxana Troi strangely appealing, which makes him unique in the universe. A bizarre conflation of attempted humor best exemplified by Marina Sirtis' masterful expressions of profound embarrassment, this episode falls with a resounding thud.

"Transfigurations" concerns a wounded, amnesiac alien with strange powers of recovery who strikes an easy rapport with Beverly Crusher. He is pursued by representatives of his culture; remembering himself, he is revealed as a person in the final stages of his race's evolution to a higher form, a metamorphosis ruthlessly suppressed by his government, but he succeeds in moving on, pointing the way for others. . .perhaps, someday, even humans.

After the dismal and cheating conclusion to season two, *The Next Generation's* producers wisely chose to end the third season with a bang-up finale. "The Best of Both Worlds" brings back the Borg, intent upon absorbing the Federation and all other life forms into their machine-hive mind.

The Enterprise responds to a distress signal from the outermost reaches of Federation space, only to find the colony and its nine hundred inhabitants missing, a vast crater where the settlement once stood. Admiral Hansen and a Commander Shelby join the Enterprise; they fear that the Borg are responsible. The Federation is not ready for the Borg.

Shelby, an ambitious woman, is gunning for Riker's first officer chair. Riker has been offered his own command for the third time, but wants to remain on the Enterprise. Friction develops between him and Shelby.

The Borg enter Federation space and destroy a ship. When the Enterprise intercepts them, they hail Picard by name, and try to pull the Enterprise in with a tractor beam. They manage to break free with difficulty, for the Borg adapt quickly to any change in phaser frequency or shield harmonics.

Picard steers the ship into a nebula cloud, but the Borg bombard it and drive him back out. Another attack ensues, during which several Borg appear on the bridge and kidnap Picard. Once they have him, they ignore the Enterprise and head towards the heart of the Federation— Earth.

Riker becomes acting commander of the Enterprise. He plans to attack the Borg ship with a concentrated phaser burst through the deflector shield.

An away team led by Shelby beams onto the Borg ship and disrupt systems causing the ship to drop out of warp. They also discover that Picard has become a Borg before they beam back to the Enterprise.

Picard, now a Borg called Locutus, has been chosen to speak for the Borg. He demands that the Enterprise surrender. Riker, faced with what his former captain has become, gives Worf the order to fire on the Borg ship.

This cliffhanger ending left audiences clamoring for more, which was a shrewd move after the two lame-duck season finales that preceded it. It was a long summer after "The Best of Both Worlds" brought the season to its end; there was little else for captivated viewers to do but to watch reruns of *The Next Generation* until fall. Where Kirk and crew had slipped on a banana peel the pre-

vious summer, Riker, Data, Worf and their cohorts seemed bound to fly even higher than
ever— with or without Picard. (Supposedly, Patrick Stewart was considering leaving the show—
the cliffhanger gave him time to reconsider, it
seems.) To top off everything, the fourth season
would take the episode count of *The Next Generation* beyond the seventy-nine show record of
its illustrious predecessor, a sure sign that the end
was not in sight.

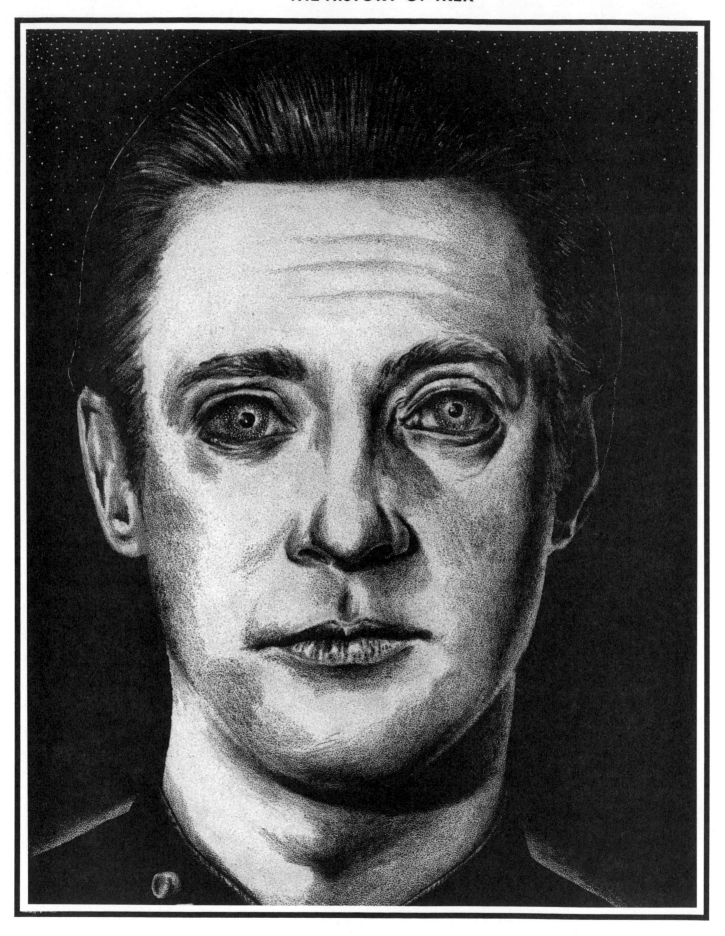

CHAPTER TEN:

THE TORCH IS CARRIED ON

The Next Generation's 1990 season got off to a rousing start with the conclusion to the cliffhanger ending of season three. The special effects team had to dust off the six-foot Enterprise for a saucer separation sequence, but this was the least of their triumphs in the opening episode.

The attack on the Borg ship fails, causing extensive systems damage to the Enterprise. The Borg, having absorbed Picard into their group mind, now possess all his knowledge and experience, and resume their course to Earth.

Admiral Hansen communicates with the Enterprise: the Federation has assembled an armada of forty of their own ships, in addition to the Klingons. They are even considering contacting the Romulans. Riker receives a field commission, and promises to join the Federation forces as soon as the Enterprise is functional again. Shelby becomes First Officer.

Hansen communicates again: the Federation has engaged the Borg, and the battle is not going well. His transmission is cut off abruptly. When the Enterprise reaches the battle site, they find a scene of complete devastation.

Riker plans to separate the saucer section of the Enterprise for a diversion. Picard knew of this plan, but Riker has altered it considerably, hoping to outwit the memories of his former mentor.

The Borg ship's magnetic field now blocks transporter beams, so Worf and Data take a shuttle into range and use its escape transport to beam onto the Borg ship and recapture Picard/Locutus. They return to the shuttle, clear the Borg field, and beam back to the Enterprise just before the shuttle is destroyed. The two ship sections reconnect.

Picard/Locutus is still linked by subspace signal with the Borg mind.

Data creates a neural link with Picard/Locutus, and eventually reaches the Borg command system. It is divided into various command sub-units, but he cannot access any of the vital areas. The Borg halt their advance on Earth and attack the Enterprise; Riker orders a last-ditch, warp-speed collision with the Borg ship.

Picard's personality emerges, and repeats the word "sleep." Crusher takes this as an expression of fatigue, but Data realizes that Picard is telling him what to do: the Borg regenerative system is of low priority, easily accessed, and Data uses it to convince the Borg that it is time for a regenerative cycle, effectively putting them all to sleep.

The Borg attack stops. A power feedback caused by this induced malfunction causes the Borg ship to self-destruct, freeing Picard from their subspace link. The Borg machinery is removed from his body. The Enterprise docks for repair, and Shelby leaves to head the task force rebuilding the fleet.

"Family" is a direct follow-up to the preceding episode, as a weary Jean-Luc Picard takes some time off at his family estate in France and works out some long standing grudges with his older brother, a gruff farmer. Wesley finally meets his father via a recorded holodeck message, and Worf is embarrassed when his human foster parents come on board the Enterprise. An intriguing character study, this episode works admirably without any life threatening crises whatsoever.

"Brothers" opens with Data suddenly shifting into a mysterious mode and taking over the Enterprise, diverting it to a mysterious planet, and beaming down, leaving a bewildered crew striving to figure out the complex code he entered into the computer— using Picard's voice!

On the planet's surface, Data encounters an aged human who turns out to be Dr. Noonian Soong, Data's creator. Soong has long been presumed dead but actually fled the events described in the first season's "Datalore" and escaped to this distant hideout.

Now he is dying, and has called Data there to give him a new, improved chip that will provide him with basic emotions; his first attempt, with "evil twin" Lore didn't work out. Lore himself shows up, since the homing signal also triggered him. Lore is jealous of the attention Data is getting, and tricks Soong into giving him the chip, which causes him to become even more twisted.

Soong dies after being manhandled by Lore, leaving Data no better off than before, and the Enterprise is restored to Picard. Some but not all of the discrepancies between the information in this episode and "Datalore" can be attributed to the fact that Lore is a liar.

Originally, this story merely had Data meeting his creator until Michael Piller realized that that provided a rather static scenario, and so he brought back Lore to spice up the proceedings. Veteran actor Keye Luke, since deceased, was considered for the role of Soongh but it was decided to give Brent Spiner all three roles: a more expensive approach, to be sure, but one that made this a tour-de-force for the Texan actor.

"Suddenly Human" draws Picard into controversy when he discovers that a teenager found on a damaged alien craft is actually human. Picard tries to reacclimate the boy to human society but it's a losing battle, with humorous overtones deriving from the Captain's faltering attempts to be a surrogate father.

The boy's Tellarian foster father tries to reclaim him, but old injuries revealed by a medical scan lead Picard and crew to assume the possibility of abuse, a touchy issue skirted around, used here basically to provide a stalling device, rather than have the youth simply handed over to the culture where he belongs. Anyway, it all works out in the end, as the boy decides to continue his life as a Tellarian.

"Remember Me" traps Dr. Crusher on an Enterprise where the crew is disappearing, but no one notices but her. Eventually, she and Picard are alone on the bridge, and the Captain is reduced to patiently explaining to her that the two of them are all the crew that the ship requires. Actually, she has been trapped in a warp bubble produced by an experiment of her son, who is desperately trying to save her. As the bubble collapses, Crusher, now alone, finds that the universe around her is shrinking, shearing away sections of the false reality she inhabits.

Suspecting the truth, she struggles to get to the engineering section of the construct before it is lost. Wesley's efforts are aided by the arrival of the Traveller from the first season's "Where No One Has Gone Before," who joins Wesley in saving his mother; Wesley actually 'phases out' at the controls, as the Traveller once did, and all is set right.

"Legacy" takes the Enterprise to Tasha Yar's home world to rescue some captured Federation officers. They are drawn into that planet's long-standing factional war, which has achieved a sort of balance of power which both sides desire to break. One side has a trump card designed to win the help of the Enterprise crew, especially Data: Tasha Yar's sister Ishara, who uses the trusting android and almost succeeds in her plan. Effective in that a viable friendship between Yar and Data is destroyed by her previous allegiance to her cause. She is left behind after the hostages are liberated.

"Reunion" brings back Worf's gal K'Ehleyr and continues the Klingon saga. A Klingon cruiser hails the Enterprise. Worf's old flame K'Ehleyr beams over with a message for Picard: the leader of the Klingon High Council is dying, and wants Picard to discover which of the contenders for his position has been poisoning.

K'Ehleyr also has a surprise for Worf: their last encounter produced a son, Alexander. K'Ehleyr is now willing to make the marriage vows she earlier declined, but Worf resists because of his discommendation.

The two Klingon contenders arrive, and discover that Picard has been chosen by the late Klingon leader as the arbitrator, who determines the challenger's right to battle for the Ascension. At the preliminary ritual, a bomb goes off, killing two Klingon aides. Picard delays further ceremonies by insisting on an archaic ritual which demands a long recitation of the challengers' accomplishments, a ritual which could take hours or days.

The Enterprise crew determines that the bomb was a sort used only by the Romulans, and that it was implanted in the forearm of the aide of one of the challengers: Worf's old enemy, the Klingon responsible for Worf's family dishonor. It seems that he, like his father, is a traitor, doing business with the Romulans.

As this goes on, K'Ehleyr tries to discover the reasons for Worf's discommendation, which neither Worf nor Captain Picard will reveal to her. She manages to put together the truth, but she is discovered and killed by the traitor.

Worf discovers her body and beams over to the Klingon's ship, claiming right of revenge. His claim is questioned until he reveals that K'Ehleyr was his mate; he fights his enemy to the death, triumphing over him seconds before a security teams arrives to escort him back to the Enterprise. (Apparently, right of vengeance outweighs dishonor in Klingon ethics.)

The Klingon High Council approves Worf's action, since the Klingon he killed was revealed as a traitor. Picard takes him to task, but all he will receive in punishment is a reprimand on his record. Although his enemy is dead, Worf must keep the truth behind his dishonor a secret until the time is right for him and his brother to set matters right.

"Future Imperfect" finds Riker awakening after sixteen years to find himself the captain of the Enterprise, with a son. He has forgotten the sixteen years in question; his last memory is of a visit to a planet, where he was infected by a virus that lay dormant for years until wiping out all memories accrued since its inception.

On the verge of an important diplomatic mission, he is hard pressed to deal with this 'new' reality. The computer is slow to provide records of his missing years, especially those concerning his late wife; when at last he is shown home videos of her, she turns out to be Minuet, the holodeck creation from the first season's "11001001."

This reveals that this is all a sham, and he faces down a bearded Admiral Picard. The bridge fades away, revealed to be a Romulan holodeck simulation set up in order to extract information from Riker. His 'son' is revealed to be a captured Earth boy. Another adventure ensues, but it too begins to show gaps in its consistency, and Riker realizes that he's being duped again.

The boy is revealed to be an alien child, hidden from enemies by his late parents; the devices they provided him for his protection have also enabled him to create illusions that will enable him to trick Riker into being his friend. But Riker, faced with the truth, takes the child with him, ending his lonely exile. It seems he was the right choice for a friend after all.

"Final Mission" is Will Wheaton's farewell as Wesley Crusher; he and Picard are stranded on a desert world, Picard is wounded, and Wesley must take charge to save the Captain's life. The following episode, "The Loss," deprives Deanna Troi of her empathic powers. Although it's a forgone conclusion that she'll get them back within the hour, she does go through some interesting emotional situations in a dramatically interesting script.

"Data's Day" is a busy one: In order to help Commander Maddox better understand him, Data sends him a communication describing a "typical" day in the life of the android. On the day in question, Data is to act as father of the bride in the wedding of Keiko to Chief O'Brien.

When Keiko calls the wedding off, Data misgauges the effect that the news will have on O'Brien. He also has a long way to go in learning the use of friendly jibes and insults, although he does not offend Geordi when he calls him 'a lunkhead.'

When Geordi assures him that Keiko will change her mind again, Data resumes his preparations for the wedding, and arranges for Doctor Crusher to give him dancing lessons, since her records indicate that she won a dance competition many years earlier. It is also revealed that Data keeps a pet cat in his quarters.

Vulcan Ambassador T'Pel beams aboard to meet Picard; she is on a mission of utmost secrecy, one which will take them into the Neutral Zone.

The Ambassador queries Data about the Enterprise's security. Although she has the correct clearance codes, he tells her he must inform Picard; she withdraws the question, claiming that is was merely a test of his own security precautions.

T'Pel's mission brings the Enterprise face-to-face with a Romulan warbird. She beams over to begin secret negotiations, but a transporter accident kills her, leaving only minute organic traces on the transporter pad. The Enterprise leaves, but investigations reveal that the traces do not correspond with the records from when T'Pel beamed aboard. The Romulans somehow managed to alter their own transporters to fake T'Pel's death.

Picard pursues them and demands the Ambassador's return, only to the discover that she was not a Vulcan after all, but a well-placed Romulan spy.

The Enterprise heads back to Federation space.

The wedding goes on as planned, in a traditional Japanese ceremony officiated by Captain Picard. Data has learned a little more about humans, although he has also gained more questions to be answered about them as well.

The following episode, "The Wounded," was also an intriguing story. While surveying a sector near the space of Federation enemies-turned-allies, the Kardassians, the Enterprise is fired on by a Kardassian ship. After a brief exchange of fire, Picard discovers that the peace has been broken by the Federation ship Phoenix, commanded by Ben Maxwell.

Maxwell has been out of communication for some time, and is apparently acting on his own initiative: the Phoenix has destroyed a Kardassian science station without provocation. The Federation orders Picard to investigate, and to take a Kardassian team aboard as observers.

This brings up memories for chief O'Brien, who served with Maxwell in the conflict with the Kardassians. Maxwell lost his family in a border skirmish, which may account for his actions, while O'Brien recalls a battle in which he killed a Kardassian to save his own life. He has trouble dealing with Kardassians on board, not because he hates them, but because they remind him of his only act of aggression against another living being.

The Enterprise's sensors locate the Phoenix in time to watch it destroy a Kardassian warship and freighter. Pursuing at high speed, they catch up, and discover that Maxwell believes the Kardassians to be re-arming. He agrees to return to Federation space, and Picard allows him to keep command of the Phoenix.

Maxwell soon breaks away and heads toward another Kardassian freighter. If Picard will not board the freighter and see that Maxwell is right, then Maxwell will fire upon it. Picard in turn threatens to use force against the Phoenix.

O'Brien uses his expertise to beam over through a cyclic break in the Phoenix's shields, and talks to the unhinged Maxwell, reviewing their past together and helping Maxwell back down from his dangerous position. Maxwell surrenders. When the Kardassian captain thanks Picard, Picard reveals that he believes Maxwell's claims, but acted as he did to preserve the peace. In parting, he warns the Kardassian that the Federation will be keeping an eye on them.

"The Devil's Due" is owed by the people of the planet Ventax to an entity named Ardra, who provided their once crisis-wracked world with peace and prosperity a thousand years ago; now that the term is up, Ardra appears, replete with earthquakes and shapeshifting powers.

Picard must prove that she's a fraud, using an ancient social myth for her own ends by taking it literally and scaring the wits out of the Ventaxians. Fortunately, her cloaked ship, with its tractor beams (for the earthquakes) and transporter (for the shape-changing) is discovered and boarded, enabling Picard to briefly assume the interplanetary conwoman's apparent powers long enough to turn the tables and thwart her greedy plan.

"Clues" leaves the Enterprise crew with a mystery: how did they lose twenty-four hours? Data knows, but he's not telling. In fact, it takes some time for them to realize the loss, and the fact that Data is concealing the truth from them. When asked why he's doing this, the android reveals the startling truth that he is acting under orders from Picard. . . orders that the Captain does not remember giving.

Ultimately, it turns out that Picard had agreed to this peculiar arrangement to protect the privacy of a reclusive alien race; he even agrees to it a second time, but cautions the aliens to destroy all traces of their passing; the first time, there were too many clues to lead the crew to suspect something was amiss. The second coverup is successful.

"First Contact" breaks with the series format to provide a startling look at the questions raised by the Federation's techniques of determining a planet's worthiness to join. Here, we see the Enterprise crew as aliens, from the Malkorian's point of view.

The Federation is secretly studying Malkorian society, which is on the verge of achieving interstellar flight. Riker, altered to resemble a Malkorian, is injured and taken to a hospital, where it soon becomes apparent that he is not what he appears to be: his organs are in the wrong places, and certain features are surgical implants.

He claims that they are hereditary defects, and that his phaser is a toy for a neighbor's child, but the doctor treating him is not convinced. To make matters worse, Riker's communicator is lost.

Picard takes a chance and beams down with Deanna to reveal himself to the Malkorian Science Minister, Mirasta, a forward-looking woman who is largely responsible for her world's great leaps towards warp technology. She is open minded, and visits the Enterprise, but points out that her culture is very conservative and ethnocentric, believing themselves to be the center of the universe. The planetary Chancellor is fair-minded if cautious, but the Security Minister, Krolar, is a fanatic about his traditional way of life.

The doctor treating Riker is dedicated to helping him recover, but his efforts at keeping the strange facts of Riker's case quiet fail, and word of the alien soon spreads through the hospital.

Mirasta and Picard beam down to the Chancellor's office. The Chancellor is skeptical of the Federation's aims, but Picard wins his respect. On Mirasta's advice, however, he does not mention the covert survey teams.

The Chancellor tours the Enterprise, where he and Picard share a toast with the wine given Picard by his brother on his last visit to Earth. Still, the Chancellor is uncertain what to do.

Riker is visited by a nurse, Lanel, who is fascinated by the idea of aliens. Since this seems to be the key to getting her help, Riker, somewhat humorously, admits that he's an alien. Lanel offers to help him escape if he will make love to her— making love with an alien has long been her fantasy!

Later, when Riker tries to slip out of the hospital, he is detected, and mobbed by a frightened crowd. He suffers kidney damage and internal bleeding, and is taken into intensive care, where the doctor struggles to help him.

The Chancellor discusses the situation with his ministers. Krolar is not only the most resistant to the idea, he also has word of a spy, presently in the hospital. The Chancellor is disturbed to learn of the covert operation.

Krolar takes matters into his own hands, and goes to the hospital to interrogate Riker, whom he believes represents an invading force. Krolar orders the doctor to awaken Riker, but the doctor refuses, because the stimulants could prove fatal. Krolar uses his influence to have the doctor removed as head of the hospital, and his ambitious replacement is all too anxious to follow Krolars orders.

Once Riker regains consciousness, Krolar arranges to be alone with him. He has discovered how to operate the phaser, and places it in Riker's hand, intending to kill himself while making it look like murder. His death will put an end to any notion of contact with aliens. Riker struggles to keep the phaser from firing, but Krolar succeeds in triggering it, and is blasted across the room.

The phaser discharge gives the Enterprise a fix on Riker, and Crusher and a medical team beam down to the hospital in time to save both Riker and Krolar, who did not realize that the phaser was set on stun.

Krolar survives, and awakens in the Enterprise's sick bay. His plan is easily deduced, and the Chancellor chides him for such a foolhardy undertaking. Still, it has become apparent that his world is not yet ready to make contact with other worlds, and he asks Picard to leave. The entire affair will be hushed up, and funds will be diverted from technology to education in order to help eradicate ancient prejudices.

Mirasta, who has long dreamed of space travel, asks to be taken with the Enterprise, and Picard and the Chancellor agree, since she would now be subject to to many restrictions on her home world. All that will remain of this first contact will be rumors, which, the Chancellor imagines, will fade in time.

"Galaxy's Child" primarily involves a space-bred infant that imprints on the Enterprise after its mother is inadvertently killed; it attaches itself to the ship and begins to drain power at an enormous rate. Meanwhile, Leah Brahms, who Geordi "met" on the holodeck in the previous season's "Booby Trap," visits the ship to see her engine designs in operation. She is perplexed but intrigued by Geordi's modifications, as well as by his manner, while Geordi is baffled by the fact

that she is nothing like the simulation he worked with. Not only that. . . she's married. When she discovers the holodeck program with her image in it, she goes into a rage. Fortunately, she and Geordi become friends in time to work together and resolve the episode's other plot concerns.

"Night Terrors" has the ship's crew going nuts due to sleep deprivation caused by an alien vessel's attempts to communicate telepathically; once Deanna figures out what's going on, it's a piece of cake for the Enterprise and the aliens to escape from the space anomaly holding them both captive.

"Identity Crisis" takes Geordi back to a planet he visited as part of an Away Team from the U.S.S. Victory five years before; members of that away team have been vanishing and seem to be headed back to that particular world. Geordi and Susanna, the only other Away Team member remaining, review the mission records to find out clues, but to little avail.

Susanna transforms into an alien being but is taken to sick bay; when Geordi changes, he escapes and heads down to the planet. A search ensues, while Crusher tries to isolate the cause of the metamorphosis. Unfortunately, any suspense is undercut by the certainty that Geordi will be saved by episode's end.

"The Nth Degree" features the return of Reginald Barclay, who, having recovered from holodeck addiction, is made a super intellect by an alien probe. His mind expands into the ship's computer and takes charge, taking the Enterprise to the center of the galaxy. He is restored to normalcy by a galactic being who explores the universe by having other beings visit him. The payoff is weak, but Dwight Schultz is fun as Barclay, gaining immeasurable confidence, becoming a great actor, making a play for Deanna Troi, and arguing successfully with a holodeck Albert Einstein.

"Q-Pid" features the return of Vash, Captain Picard's romantic interest from "Captain's Holiday". The captain is a bit abashed to find her part of an archaeological symposium on the Enterprise, and she is annoyed to find that he's kept mum about their affair to his fellow officers.

Into this volatile situation pops Q, who feel that he owes Picard a favor from their last encounter.

Q thus whisks Picard and crew off to a simulated recreation of the Robin Hood story (it was, after all, the summer of *Prince of Thieves*) where Vash becomes Maid Marian, due to be executed by the Sheriff of Nottingham.

Picard, a reluctant Robin Hood, must rescue her; neither the captain nor Q have taken into account Vash's keen survival instincts, and discover that she's playing along with the Sheriff's marriage plans! Q, fascinated, refuses to interfere before the situation runs its course.

Fortunately, after Picard is captured, the rest of "The Merry Men" stage a rousing escape and Picard gets to duel the villain to the death. Q restores things to normal, and announces that he's found a kindred spirit in Vash; the two don safari garb and blink away to explore the universe courtesy of Q's cosmic powers. An extremely silly episode, but the cast obviously had fun, and it shows through.

"The Drumhead," Jonathan Frakes' third directorial outing, not only makes more references to *The Next Generation's* back history, it even enumerates the number of times Picard has violated the Prime Directive. A highly effective "bottle show," it never leaves the ship, but achieves high dramatic levels.

As the story begins, a Klingon exchange officer, J'Dan, has been caught accessing security codes, and is believed to be a spy when the Romulans obtain secret information concerning the dilithium chambers. One of the chambers explodes, raising the possibility of sabotage, but J'Dan denies all charges. Deanna senses that he is lying. J'Dan offers to help clear Worf's family name in exchange for a shuttle craft, but Worf turns down the offer with a few Klingon body blows.

Starfleet calls retired Admiral Satie in to investigate the situation. The daughter of an important Federation lawmaker, she brings along two aides, including a full Betazoid, Sabin. The damaged area can't be examined until radiation levels drop, so they can only interrogate J'Dan again.

The Klingon allegedly needed injections for a certain disease, but Worf discovers that his hypo has been converted so that it can read isolinear chips. Converting the information into amino acid sequences, the device can be used to inject the information into someone's blood. Faced with this, J'Dan admits his spying, but denies having sabotaged the dilithium chambers. Sabin believes this to be true. But how did the information leave the ship? Satie suspects a conspiracy.

She soon focuses her attention on a medical crewman, Simon Tarses, who helped J'Dan with his injections. Born on the Mars colony, Tarses is mostly human but says that his paternal grandfather was a Vulcan, a claim which would explain his elongated ears. Sabin senses that Tarses is lying about something, and suspicion begins to build.

When the radiation levels drop, Geordi discovers that there was no sabotage. The explosion was just the result of subatomic material fatigue.

This does not slow Satie's investigations, which begin to develop a life of their own. A hearing convenes, with Riker as defense, and Tarses is hammered with questions. Satie demands the names of anyone J'Dan talked to in Ten Forward.

Sabin falsely suggests that the explosion was caused by a corrosive chemical. Tarse is completely off guard when he is accused of lying about his grandfather, who was really a Romulan. On Riker's advice, Tarses refuses to answer under the Seventh Guarantee, the Federation equivalent of the Fifth Amendment.

Picard warns Worf, who is an enthusiastic supporter of Satie, that things may be getting out of hand. He tells him about the drumhead trials of the 19th Century, when military officers in the field would sit on an inverted drumhead and dispense summary justice, with no right of appeal. The Captain then talks to Tarses, who admits that he lied about his ancestry for fear of prejudice. Now his career seems to be completely ruined.

Picard confronts Satie, who defends the lie about the explosion as a useful tactic. She reveals herself as a self-important chauvinist for the Federation, and accuses Picard of blocking her investigation. She has already gone over Picard's head, and called more hearings. Admiral Henry of Starfleet Security will be taking part as well. Picard vows to fight her all the way.

Later, Picard receives a command from Satie to report for questioning at the next hearing.

At the hearing, Picard requests to make an opening statement. Satie refuses him this request, but he is ready for her, and invokes the specific regulation that guarantees this. He questions the entire proceeding, and asks that it end before it hurts anyone else.

Satie attacks him, noting that he has violated the Prime Directive nine times while commanding the Enterprise. She suggests that his involvement in the affair of the Romulan spy T'Pel ("Data's Day," episode 83) was less than innocent. When Worf rises to his captain's defense, his father's alleged treachery— a rumor that has reached the Federation— is raised against him.

Satie returns to her attack on Picard and brings up his capture and use by the Borg, and all but accuses him of being responsible for the loss of 39 ships in that conflict.

Picard keeps himself in control and quotes from writings about freedom, which regard as evil the very practices Satie is using. Satie tries to shut him up, but not before he reveals that these words were written by her father.

Satie rises to her feet and demands that Picard not sully her father's name. She loses control completely, and threatens to destroy Picard, accusing him of being in on her imagined conspiracy. Admiral Henry rises without a word and walks out of the room. Sabin calls a recess. Everyone leaves the room, including Sabin, leaving Admiral Satie standing alone.

The hearings are terminated, and Satie leaves the ship, having revealed her obsessed and unstable nature. In the end, the only reputation she ruined was her own. This episode demonstrates the type of drama that *The Next Generation* was willing to explore and how different it really is from the sixties *Star Trek*.

"Half A Life" gives Majel Barrett a chance to play Lwaxana Troi as something other that a sex crazed buffoon, and the result is a very touching episode. Still chasing men, of course, she falls for the alien scientist Timicin (David Ogden Stiers of *M*A*S*H* fame), who is using the Enterprise's photon technology to test his plan to re-energize his planet's fading sun.

They become close, but when the test fails, he must return to his planet; his sixtieth birthday is approaching, and death is compulsory at that age for everyone on that world. He is anguished, since his work must be continued by people who might need years to learn how to pick up where he left off.

Lwaxana convinces him that he doesn't have to follow tradition, and his decision to stay with her creates conflicts with his world, his family, and within himself. Ultimately, he decides to honor the traditions he was raised in, and Lwaxana bravely decides to accompany him to his farewell ceremony.

"The Host," unknown to Beverly Crusher, is the body of her newfound lover Odan, an alien ambassador embarked on a vital diplomatic mission that only he can carry off. Odan himself, however, is a parasitic being that uses the humanoid body as a vehicle.

When the body sickens and dies, the truth is revealed, and Beverly transfers Odan to the body of a volunteer— Riker— until a host from his home world can arrive. This is, of course, a great strain on Riker's body, as his personality is submerged beneath that of Odan— who still proclaims his love for Beverly.

She can't accept this turn of events and avoids Odan/Riker, until she can no longer reject him, and they embrace right before a strategically placed commercial break. Needless to say, the negotiations succeed and a host body arrives in time to save Riker. When it turns out to be a female body, Beverly must break off relations again, as all these body changes are beginning to bewilder her.

This is a very intelligent, well done episode which seems to cop out at the end. Of course, it is understandable that the situation is stressful— but she's already made love to Odan using Riker's body. And this is never touched upon later— wouldn't this be a violation of Riker's privacy? Does he ever find out? How does he feel about it? And the final rejection in a way points up the fact that *Star Trek's* morality is still seen through the veil of Twentieth Century biases and opinions.

One interesting technical aspect of this episode, incidentally, is that it had to be shot in such a manner as to conceal the fact that Gates McFadden was pregnant at the time.

"The Mind's Eye" has Geordi kidnapped by Romulans and brainwashed while an impostor takes his place at a conference. When he returns from his "vacation,' he has false memories of a wonderful time behind him— and a mission to kill a Klingon governor, part of a plot to undermine Klingon/ Federation relations.

Fortunately, Data picks up the subspace transmissions controlling Geordi and manages to piece together the situation, stopping the assassination just in the nick of time. Data even narrows the choice of Geordi's controllers to two suspects: Picard or Klingon ambassador Kell.

Picard gracefully offers to submit to a search for a personal subspace transmitter, but the Klingon, unwisely refuses, and asks Picard for asylum when he realizes that he's sunk. Picard also agrees to this request— but only after the other Klingons present have determined that the ambassador is, in fact, telling the truth.

This episode featured a brand-new, never before seen Romulan ship, which would appear once more in the season finale.

Astute listeners of the show undoubtedly identified the voice of the Romulan mastermind lurking in the shadows during Geordi's brainwashing sequences— it was Denise Crosby.

"In Theory" details Data's first serious attempt at a romantic relationship when cadet Jenna falls for him on the rebound. Determined to discover the intricacies of human relationships, Data (remember, he's "fully functional") plunges into uncharted territories certain that the maps he has (complete files on the literature of romance, among other things) will show him the way.

Unfortunately, it doesn't work out; Jenna herself is too immature to cut any slack for any of the vast gaps in Data's understanding. When the relationship goes sour he begins to quote old movies and sitcoms— he even enters calling out "Honey, I'm home!"— which at least gives some insight into what remains of 20th century culture in the 24th.

A ship-threatening subplot detracts from the main storyline, which is strangely disappointing for a Data-centered story. Brent Spiner is as good as usual, of course, and Michele Scarbelli is fine as the lovesick Jenna. First-time director Patrick Stewart does at the least an adequate job on this episode.

"Redemption" is finally made available to Worf, but under rather trying circumstances. Picard still can't shake his involvement in Klingon politics. As the official Arbiter of Succession, he must go to the Klingon home world to install Gowron as head of the High Council. Klingon politics are in a bit of turmoil; Duras' sisters, an unpleasant duo, have allegedly found Duras' son, a surly teen, and challenge Gowron's right. (They're also playing footsie with Romulans, including the one with the habit of remaining obscured by shadows.)

Worf's brother is part of a group of officers planning their own power play, but Worf throws in with Gowron and uses his seniority to pull his brother (and most of his brother's cohorts) over to his side. He does, however, wait until Gowron's back is against the wall— and he has a price. When Picard rejects the Duras family claim— their contender is young and unproven— the rest of the Council withdraws to the Duras camp at Gowron's accession, leaving the new ruler to restore Worf's family name alone.

Then, to avoid conflict of interest, Worf resigns his Starfleet commission and joins with Gowron, and receives a touching send-off by the Enterprise crew. The ship then heads out of Klingon space, off to other missions. . .

. . .but down at the Duras family home, the shadowy Romulan leader steps into the light, revealing the face of Denise Crosby, and anticipating the return of Picard at some future date, as well.

Although this lacks the heavy impact of "The Best of Both Worlds," it is a strong season ender, as Worf's departure is an emotional sequence, and his fate— along with that of Federation/ Klingon relations— remains uncertain. Even the anticlimactic nature of his restoration of honor serves to underscore the perils that undoubtedly await him.

This is also counted as *The Next Generation's* one hundredth episode by its producers, although to arrive at this figure one must count "Encounter At Farpoint" as two episodes; in fact, there is some justification for this, as it consisted of two unrelated scenarios slapped haphazardly together. One need only reflect on that ponderous pilot episode to truly see just how far *The Next Generation* has come since its inception.

And as for Denise Crosby's sudden appearance on the scene— one can only wonder if this is a completely new character, or one with some strange link to Tasha Yar. Only the future will tell.

CHAPTER ELEVEN:

THE FUTURE BECKONS, BRIGHT AND BOLD

And so, *Star Trek*, in all its forms, continues to press on. *Star Trek VI: The Undiscovered Country,* is due for a Christmas 1991 release, and the beginning of *The Next Generation's* fifth season is not far away.

Rumors abound concerning all these projects. Denise Crosby's return to *The Next Generation* has led to the rather convoluted speculation that Tasha Yar somehow survived her alternative-timeline adventure in "Yesterday's Enterprise" and bore a child to a Romulan, thus providing Crosby's new character. This may explain her obsession with humans— and with Picard. This is a bit far-fetched, but stranger things can happen. One can only hope that whatever the truth is, it will be well served by *The Next Generation's* writers, who have a sterling track record to maintain.

But far from being a rumor is the news that Leonard Nimoy has signed to portray Spock (at the ripe old age of one hundred and thirty— Vulcan middle age?) in an upcoming two-part episode of *The Next Generation.*

Entitled "Unification," it promises to send Jean-Luc Picard and the Enterprise on a mission to investigate Spock's unauthorized visit to the Romulan home world. This will air in November— good timing for Paramount Studios, with their theatrical *Star Trek* film due out in December.

Interest in *Star Trek* should be at an all time high this year, with all sorts of celebrations focussing on its twenty-fifth anniversary. (The Q.V.C. Network, a shop-at-home cable service, is even having a *Star Trek* special on September 11, selling memorabilia with the help of James Doohan! The bottom line rears its head again. . .)

Indeed, Paramount, realizing that the classic crew's adventures must reach an end some day, are billing *Star Trek VI* as the last film (although the same was said about *Star Trek V*— and some actors have been signed, at least optionwise, to be in a seventh), and making certain that the public views *The Next Generation* as the continuation of the line.

And the cast of *The Next Generation,* with its contracts up after a sixth season, may well be next in line for a series of features, with yet another new crew steering the Enterprise to new adventures. That the legacy will continue cannot be doubted, for long gone are the days when *Star Trek* was considered a dubious commodity. Time and its success, especially after a few failures, have demonstrated to Paramount Pictures that *Star Trek* is a guaranteed moneymaker. This is a fact that in and of itself should assure a long line of Enterprise-related epics. All that remains is to remove any doubts concerning *The Next Generation* from the mind of the public.

Thus, the touch of legitimacy is being assured by a carefully planned crossover. Michael Dorn has a role as a Klingon lawyer in *Star Trek VI*, rumored to be Worf's grandfather. It has also long been rumored that Spock's wedding, mentioned in *The Next Generation's* "Sarek" episode, will comprise the final scene of *Star Trek VI*, and will feature a young Lieutenant Jean-Luc Picard among the wedding guests.

Leonard "Bones" McCoy has already appeared in the new series, as has Spock's father. Now Spock himself is destined to appear on the show, something which even the most chauvinistic, *Next Generation*- hating old-line fan cannot ignore. All that remains is for some mention of Kirk to be made (or perhaps one of his undoubtedly numerous offspring) to have all of the Big Three accounted for.

Star Trek VI: The Undiscovered Country should provide the topper for a seriously heavy year of *Star Trek*. Directed and written by *The Wrath of Khan's* Nicholas Meyer. It stars, in addition to the usual lineup (and Michael Dorn), Christopher Plummer as the one-eyed Klingon General Chang, and David Warner as Klingon Chancellor Gorkon.

Finding out exactly who these characters are should only be part of the adventure. All Nicholas Meyer will admit to is the fact that Spock falls in love in the movie. "That's all I'm going on record with," he says. "All Star Treks are a state secret for as long as they can be kept under wraps." Spock's romantic object would seem to be the Vulcan Lieutenant Valeris, played by Kim Cattrall; with Nimoy acting as executive producer, and providing the germ of the story, it's a sure bet that no one, not even Jim Kirk, will steal any of Spock's thunder.

It seems, after all these years, that Gene Roddenberry's impossible dream was not only highly possible— it was, perhaps inevitable. History has certainly vindicated and venerated the man dubbed "The Great Bird of the Galaxy" by the original *Star Trek* crew. The end is nowhere in sight, for now millions dream that dream. *Star Trek* will always be with us, even after we ourselves reach for the stars and beyond, inspired by these fictional yet vital pioneers.

CHECKLISTS

CLASSIC STAR TREK

FIRST SEASON (1966-67)

1. "The Man Trap"; written by George Clayton Johnson; directed by Marc Daniels

2. "Charlie X"; written by Dorothy Fontana and Gene Roddenberry; directed by Lawrence Dobkin

3. "Where No One Has Gone Before"; written by Samuel A. Peeples; directed by James Goldstone

4. "The Naked Time"; written by John D.F. Black; directed by Mark Daniels

5. "The Enemy Within"; written by Richard Matheson; directed by Leo Penn

6. "Mudd's Women"; written by Gene Roddenberry and Stephen Kandel; directed by Harvey Hart

7. "What Are Little Girls Made Of?"; written by Robert Bloch; directed by James Goldstone

8. "Miri"; written by Adrian Spies; directed by Vincent McEveety

9. "Dagger of the Mind"; written by S. Bar David (Simon Wincleberg); directed by Vincent McEveety

10. "The Corbomite Maneuver"; written by Jerry Sohl; directed by Joseph Sargent

11. "The Menagerie, Part One"; written by Gene Roddenberry; directed by Marc Daniels

12. "The Menagerie, Part Two"; written by Gene Roddenberry; directed by Robert Butler

13. "The Conscience of the King"; written by Barry Trivers; directed by Gerd Oswald

14. "Balance of Terror"; written by Paul Scneider; directed by Vincent McEveety

15. "Shore Leave; written by Theodore Sturgeon; directed by Robert Sparr

16. "The Galileo Seven"; written by Oliver Crawford and S. Bar David; directed by Robert Gist

17. "The Squire of Gothos"; written by Paul Schneider; directed by Don McDougall

18. "Arena"; written by Gene L. Coon, from the story by Fredric Brown; directed by Joseph Pevney

19. "Tomorrow Is Yesterday"; written by Dorothy Fontana; directed by Michael O'Herlihy

20. "Court Martial"; written by Don M. Mankiewics and Stephen W. Carabatsos; directed by Marc Daniels

21. "The Return of the Archons'; written by Gene Roddenberry and Boris Sobelman; directed by Joseph Pevney

22. "Space Seed"; written by Gene L. Coon and Carel Wilbur; directed by Marc Daniels

23. "A Taste of Armageddon"; written by Robert Hammer and Gene L. Coon ; directed by Joseph Pevney

24. "This Side of Paradise"; written by Nathan Butler and D.C. Fontana; directed by Ralph Senesky

25. "The Devil In The Dark"; written by Gene L. Coon; directed by [?]

26. "Errand of Mercy"; written by Gene L. Coon; directed by John Newlam

27. "The Alternative Factor"; written by Don Ingalls; directed by Gerd Oswald

28. "The City On The Edge of Forever"; written by Harlan Ellison; directed by Joseph Pevney

29. "Operation: Annihilate"; written by Stephen W. Carabatsos; directed by Herschel Daugherty

SECOND SEASON (1967-68)

30. "Amok Time"; written by Theodore Sturgeon; directed by Joseph Pevney

31. "Who Mourns For Adonis?"; written by Gilbert Ralston and Gene L. Coon; directed by Marc Daniels

32. "The Changeling"; written by John Meredyth Lucas; directed by Marc Daniels

33. "Mirror, Mirror"; written by Jerome Bixby; directed by Joseph Pevney

34. "The Apple"; written by Max Erlich; directed by Joseph Pevney

35. "The Doomsday Machine"; written by Norman Spinrad; directed by Marc Daniels

36. "Catspaw"; written by Robert Bloch; directed by Joseph Pevney

37. "I, Mudd"; written by Stephen Kandel; directed by Marc Daniels

38. "Metamorphosis"; written by Gene L. Coon; directed by Ralph Senesky

39. "Journey To Babel"; written by D.C. Fontana; directed by Joseph Pevney

40. "Friday's Child"; written by D.C. Fontana; directed by Joseph Pevney

41. "The Deadly Years"; written by David P. Harmon; directed by Joseph Pevney

42. "Obsession"; written by Art Wallace; directed by Ralph Senesky

43. "Wolf In The Fold"; written by Robert Bloch; directed by Joseph Pevney

44. "The Trouble With Tribbles"; written by David Gerrold; directed by Joseph Pevney

45. "The Gamesters of Triskelion"; written by Margaret Armen; directed by [?]

46. "A Piece of the Action"; written by David Harmon and Gene L. Coon; directed by James Komack

47. "The Immunity Syndrome"; written by Robert Sabaroff; directed by Joseph Pevney

48. "A Private Little War"; written by Judd Crucis and Gene Roddenberry; directed by Marc Daniels

49. "Return To Tomorrow"; written by John Kingsbridge; directed by Ralph Senesky

50. "Patterns of Force"; written by John Meredyth Lucas; directed by [?]

51. "By Any Other Name"; written by Jerome Bixby and D.C. Fontana; directed by Marc Daniels

52. "Omega Glory"; written by Gene Roddenberry; directed by Vincent McEveety

53. "The Ultimate Computer"; written by Lawrence Wolfe and D.C. Fontana; directed by John Meredyth Lucas

54. "Bread And Circuses"; written by John Kneubel and Gene Roddenberry; directed by Ralph Senesky

55. "Assignment: Earth"; written by Art Wallace and Gene Roddenberry; directed by Marc Daniels

THIRD SEASON (1968-69)

56. "Spock's Brain"; written by Lee Cronin; directed by Marc Daniels

57. "The Enterprise Incident"; written by D.C. Fontana; directed by [?]

58. "The Paradise Syndrome"; written by Margaret Armen; directed by Judd Taylor

59. "And The Children Shall Lead"; written by Edward J. Lasko; directed by Marvin Chomsky

60. "Is There In Truth No Beauty?"; written by Jean Lisette Aroests; directed by Ralph Senesky

61. "The Spectre of the Gun"; written by Lee Cronin (pseudonyn for Gene L. Coon); directed by Vincent McEveety

62. "Day of the Dove"; written by Jerome Bixby; directed by Marvin Chomsky

63. "For The World Is Hollow And I Have Touched The Sky"; written by Rick Vollaerts; directed by Tony Leader

64. "The Tholian Web"; written by Judy Barnes; directed by Herb Wallerstein

65. "Plato's Stepchildren"; written by Meyer Dolinsky; directed by David Alexander

66. "The Wink of An Eye"; written by Arthur Neineman and Lee Cronin; directed by Jud Taylor

67. "The Empath"; written by Joyce Muscat; directed by John Erman

68. "Elaan of Troyius"; written and directed by John Meredyth Lucas

69. "Whom Gods Destroy"; written by Lee Erwin and Jerry Sohl; directed by Herb Wallerstein

70. "Let That Be Your Last Battlefield"; written by Lee Cronin and Oliver Crawford; directed by Jud Taylor

71. "The Mark of Gideon"; written by George Slavin and Stanley Adams; directed by Jud Taylor

72. "That Which Survives"; written by D.C. Fontana and George Meredyth Lucas; directed by Michael Richards

73. "The Lights of Zetar"; written by Shari Lewis and Jerry Tarcher; directed by Herb Wallerstein

74. "Requiem For Methuselah"; written by Jerome Bixby; directed by Murray Golden

75. "The Way To Eden"; written by Michael Richards and Arthur Heineman; directed by David Alexander

76. "The Cloud Minders"; written by Oliver Crawford, Margaret Armen and David Gerrold; directed by Jud Taylor

77. "The Savage Curtain"; written by Gene Roddenberry and Arthur Heinemann; directed by Herschel Daugherty

78. "All Our Yesterdays"; written by Jean Lisette Aroeste; directed by Marvin Chomsky

79. "Turnabout Intruder"; written by Gene Roddenberry and Arthur Heinemann; directed by Herb Wallerstein

CHECKLISTS

ANIMATED STAR TREK

THE HISTORY OF TREK

1. BEYOND THE FARTHEST STAR Written by Samuel A. Peeples

2. YESTERYEAR Written by D.C. Fontana

3. ONE OF OUR PLANETS IS MISSING Written by Marc Daniels

4. THE LORELEI SIGNAL Written by Margaret Armen

5. MORE TRIBBLES, MORE TROUBLES Written by David Gerrold

6. THE SURVIVOR Written by James Schermer

7. THE INFINITE VULCAN Written by Walter Koenig

8. THE MAGICKS OF MEGAS-TU Written by Larry Brody

9. ONCE UPON A PLANET Written by Chuck Menville and Len Jansen

10. MUDD'S PASSION Written by Stephen Kandel

11. THE TERRATIN INCIDENT Written by Paul Schneider

12. THE TIME TRAP Written by Joyce Perry

13. THE AMBERGRIS ELEMENT Written by Margaret Armen

14. THE SLAVER WEAPON Written by Larry Niven (from his story The Soft Weapon)

15. THE EYE OF THE BEHOLDER Written by David P. Harmon

16. THE JIHAD Written by Stephen J. Kandel

17. THE PIRATES OF ORION Written by Howard Weinstein

18. BEM Written by David Gerrold

19. THE PRACTICAL JOKER Written by Chuck Menville

20. ALBATROSS Written by Dario Finelli

21. HOW SHARPER THAN A SERPENT'S TOOTH Written by Russel Bates and David Wise

22. THE COUNTER-CLOCK INCIDENT Written by John Culver

CHECKLISTS

THE NEXT GENERATION

SEASON ONE (1987-88)

1. ENCOUNTER AT FARPOINT (Two hours)

Written by D.C. Fontana and Gene Roddenberry; Directed by Corey Allen

Guest Cast: John deLancie ; Michael Bell; DeForest Kelley; Colm Meaney; Cary Hiroyuki ; Timothy Dang; David Erskine; Evelyn Guerrero; Chuck Hicks.

2.THE NAKED NOW

Teleplay by J. Michael Bingham; Story by John D.F. Black and J. Michael Bingham; Directed by Paul Lynch

Guest Cast: Benjamin W.S. Lum; Michael Rider; David Renan; Skip Stellrecht; Kenny Koch.

3. CODE OF HONOR

Teleplay by Kathryn Powers and Michael Baron; Directed by Russ Mayberry

Guest Cast: Jessie Lawrence Ferguson; Karole Selmon; James Louis Watkins; Michael Rider.

4. THE LAST OUTPOST

Teleplay by Herbert Wright; Story by Richard Krzemian; Directed by Richard Colla

Guest Cast: Darryl Henriques; Mike Gomez; Armin Shimerman; Jake Dengal; Tracey Walter.

5. WHERE NO ONE HAS GONE BEFORE

Written by Diane Duane and Michael Reaves; Directed by Rob Bowman

Guest Cast: Biff Yeager; Charles Dayton; Victoria Dillard; Stanley Kamel; Eric Menyuk; Herta Ware.

6. LONELY AMONG US; Script by D.C. Fontana; Story by Michael Halperin; Directed by Cliff Bole

Guest Cast: Colm Meaney; Kavi Raz; John Durbin.

7. JUSTICE

Teleplay by Worley Thorne; Story by Ralph Willis and Worley Thorne; Directed by James L. Conway

Guest Cast: Josh Clark; David Q. Combs; Richard Lavin; Judith Jones; Eric Matthew; Brad Zerbst; David Michael Graves

8. THE BATTLE

Teleplay by Herbert Wright; Story by Larry Forester; Directed by Rob Bowman

Guest Cast: Frank Corsentino; Doug Warhit; Robert Towers

9. HIDE AND Q

Teleplay by C.J. Holland and Gene Roddenberry; Story by C.J. Holland; Directed by Cliff Bole

Guest Cast: John de Lancie; Elaine Nalee; William A. Wallace

10. HAVEN

Teleplay by Tracy Torme; Story by Tracy Torme and Lian Okun; Directed by Richard Compton

Guest Cast: Danzita Kingsley; Carel Struycken; Anna Katrina; Raye Birk; Michael Rider; Majel Barrett; Rob Knepper; Nan Martin; Robert Ellenstein

11. THE BIG GOODBYE

Written by Tracy Torme; Directed by Joseph L. Scanlan

Guest Cast: Mike Genovese; Dick Miller; Carolyn Alport; Rhonda Aldrich; Eric Cord; Lawrence Tierney; Harvey Jason; William Boyett; David Selburg; Gary Armagnal

12. DATALORE

Teleplay by Robert Lewin and Gene Roddenberry; Story by Robert Lewin and Maurice Hurley; Directed by Rob Bowman

Guest Cast: Biff Yeager

13. ANGEL ONE

Teleplay by Patrick Berry; Directed by Michael Rhodes

Guest Cast: Karen Montgomery; Sam Hennings; Leonard John Crowfoot; Patricia McPherson

14. 11001001

Written by Maurice Hurley and Robert Lewin; Directed by Paul Lynch

Guest Cast: Carolyn McCormack; Iva Lane; Kelli Ann McNally; Jack Sheldon; Abdul Salaam El Razzac; Ron Brown; Gene Dynarski; Katy Boyer; Alexandra Johnson

15. TOO SHORT A SEASON

Teleplay by Michael Michaelian and D.C. Fontana; Story by Michael Michaelian; Directed by Rob Bowman

Guest Cast: Clayton Rohner; Marsha Hunt; Michael Pataki

16. WHEN THE BOUGH BREAKS

Teleplay by Hannah Louise Shearer; Directed by Kim Manners

Guest Cast: Dierk Torsek; Michele Marsh; Dan Mason; Philip N. Waller; Connie Danese; Jessica and Vanessa Bova; Jerry Hardin; Brenda Strong; Jandi Swanson; Paul Lambert; Ivy Bethune

17. HOME SOIL

Teleplay by Robert Sabaroff; Story by Karl Guers, Ralph Sanchez and Robert Sabaroff; Directed by Corey Allen

Guest Cast: Walter Gotell; Elizabeth Lidsey; Mario Roccuzzo; Carolyn Barry; Gerard Pendergast

18. COMING OF AGE

Written by Sandy Fries; Directed by Michael Vejar; Guest stars: ; Estee Chandler; Daniel Riordan; Brendan McKane; Wyatt Knight; Ward Costello; Robert Schekkan; Robert Ito; John Putch; Stephan Gregory; Tasia Valenza

19. HEART OF GLORY

Teleplay by Maurice Hurley; Story by Maurice Hurley and Herb Wright & D.C. Fontana; Directed by Rob Bowman

Guest Cast: Vaughn Armstrong; Robert Bauer; Brad Zerbst; Dennis Madalone; Charles H. Hyman

20. ARSENAL OF FREEDOM

Teleplay by Richard Manning and Hans Beimler ; Story by Maurice Hurley and Robert Lewin; Directed by Les Landau

Guest Cast: Vincent Schiavelli; Marco Rodriguez; Vyto Ruginis; Julia Nickson; George De La Pena

21. SYMBIOSIS

Teleplay by Robert Lewin, Richard Manning, and Hans Beimler; Story by Robert Lewin; Directed by Win Phelps

Guest Cast: Merritt Butrick; Kimberly Farr; Richard Lineback

22. SKIN OF EVIL

Teleplay by Joseph Stephano and Hannah Louise Shearer; Story by Joseph Stephano; Directed by Joseph L. Scanlan

Guest Cast: Ron Gans as the voice of Armus; Walker Boone; Brad Zerbst; Raymond Forchion; Mart McChesney

23. WE'LL ALWAYS HAVE PARIS

Teleplay by Deaborah Dean Davis and Hannah Louise Shearer; Directed by Robert Becker; Guest stars:; Isabel Lorca; Rod Loomis; Dan Kern; Jean-Paul Vignon; Kelly Ashmore; Lance Spellerberg; Michelle Phillips

24. CONSPIRACY

Teleplay by Tracy Torme; Story by Robert Sabaroff; Directed by Cliff Bole; Guest cast;; Michael Berryman; Ursaline Bryant; Henry Darrow; Robert Schenkkan; Jonathan Farwell

25. THE NEUTRAL ZONE; Television story and teleplay by Maurice Hurley; From a story by Deborah McIntyre and Mona Clee; Directed by James L. Conway

SEASON TWO (1988-89)

26. THE CHILD

Written by Jaron Summer, Jon Povil and Maurice Hurley; Directed by Rob Bowman

Guest Cast: Seymour Cassel

27. WHERE SILENCE HAS LEASE

Written by Jack B. Sowards; Directed by Winrich Kolbe

Guest Cast: Earl Boen

28. ELEMENTARY, DEAR DATA

Written by Brian Alan Lane; Directed by Rob Bowman

Guest Cast: Daniel Davis; Alan Shearman

29. THE OUTRAGEOUS OKONA

Teleplay by Burton Armus; Story by Les Menchen, Lance Dickson and Kieran Mulroney [double-check]; Directed by Robert Becker

Guest Cast: William O. Campbell; Douglas Rowe; Albert Stratton; Joe Piscopo

; 30. LOUD AS A WHISPER

Written by Jacqueline Zambrano; Directed by Larry Shaw

Guest Cast: Howie Seago; Marnie Mosiman; Thomas Oglesby; Leo Damian

31. UNNATURAL SELECTION

Written by John Mason and Mike Gray; Directed by Paul Lynch

Guest Cast: Patricia Smith; J. Patrick McNamara; Scott Trost

32. A MATTER OF HONOR

Teleplay by Burton Armus; Story by Wanda M. Haight, Gregory Amos and Burton Armus; Directed by Rob Bowman

Guest Cast: John Putch; Christopher Collins; Brian Thompson

33. THE MEASURE OF A MAN

Written by Melinda M. Snodgrass; Directed by Robert Scheerer

Guest Cast: Amanda McBroom; Clyde Kusatsu; Brian Brophy

34. THE SCHIZOID MAN

Teleplay by Tracy Torme; Story by Richard Manning and Hans Beimler; Directed by Les Landau

Guest Cast: W. Morgan Sheppard; Suzie Plakson; Barbara Alyn Woods

35. THE DAUPHIN

Written by Scott Rubinstein and Leonard Mlodinow; Directed by Rob Bowman

Guest Cast: Paddi Edwards ; Jamie Hubbard; Madchen Amick; Cindy Sorenson; Jennifer Barlow

36. CONTAGION

Written by Steve Gerber and Beth Woods; Directed by Joseph L. Scanlan

Guest Cast: Thalmus Rasulala; Carolyn Seymour; Dana Sparks

37. THE ROYALE

Written by Keith Mills; Directed by Cliff Bole

Guest Cast: Sam Anderson; Jill Jacobson; Leo Garcia; Noble Willingham

38. TIME SQUARED

Teleplay by Maurice Hurley; Story by Kurt Michael Bensmiller; Directed by Joseph L. Scanlan

39. THE ICARUS FACTOR

Teleplay by David Assael and Robert L. McCullough; Story by David Assael; Directed by Robert Iscove

Guest Cast: Mitchell Ryan

40. PEN PALS

Teleplay by Melinda M. Snodgrass; Story by Hannah Louise Shearer; Directed by Winrich Kolbe

Guest Cast: Nicholas Cascone; Nikki Cox; Ann H. Gillespie; Whitney Rydbeck

41. Q WHO

Written by Maurice Hurley; Directed by Rob Bowman

Guest Cast: John DeLancie; Lycia Naff

42. SAMARITAN SNARE

Written by Robert L. McCullough; Directed by Les Landau

Guest Cast: Christopher Collins; Leslie Morris; Daniel Bemzau; Lycia Naff; Tzi Ma

43. UP THE LONG LADDER

Written by Melinda M. Snodgrass; Directed by Winrich Kolbe

Guest Cast: Barrie Ingham; Jon deVries; Rosalyn Landor

44. MANHUNT

Written by Terry Devereaux; Directed by Rob Bowman

Guest Cast: Majel Barrett; Robert Costanzo; Rod Arrants; Carel Struycken; Robert O'Reilly; Rhonda Aldrich; Mick Fleetwood

45. THE EMISSARY; Television story and teleplay by Richard Manning and Hans Beimler; Based on an unpublished story by Thomas H. Calder; Directed by Cliff Bole

Guest Cast: Suzie Plakson; Lance LeGault; Georgann Johnson

46. PEAK PERFORMANCE

Written by David Kemper; Directed by Robert Scheerer

Guest Cast: Roy Brocksmith; Armin Shimerman; David L. Lander;   ; 47. SHADES OF GREY

Teleplay by Maurice Hurley, Richard Manning and Hans Beimler; Story by Maurice Hurley; Directed by Rob Bowman

SEASON THREE (1989-90)

; 48. EVOLUTION

Teleplay by Michael Piller; Story by Michael Piller and Michael Wagner; Directed by Winrich Kolbe

49. THE ENSIGNS OF COMMAND

Written by Melinda M. Snodgrass; Directed by Cliff Bole

Guest Cast: Eileen Seeley; Mark L. Taylor; Richard Allen

50. THE SURVIVORS

Written by Michael Wagner; Directed by Les Landau

Guest Cast: John Anderson; Anne Haney

51. WHO WATCHES THE WATCHERS

Written by Richard Manning and Hans Beimler; Directed by Robert Weimer

Guest Cast: Kathryn Leigh Scott; Ray Wise; James Greene; Pamela Segaul; John McLiam

52. THE BONDING

Written by Ronald D. Moore; Directed by Winrich Kolbe

Guest Cast: Susan Powell; Gabriel Damon

53. BOOBY TRAP

Written by Ron Roman, Michael Pilar, Richard Danus and Michael Wagner; Diredted by Gabrielle Beaumont

Guest Cast: Susan Gibney

54. THE ENEMY

Written by David Kemper and Michael Piller; Directed by David Carson

Guest Cast: John Snyder; Andreas Katsulas; Steve Rankin

55. THE PRICE

Written by Hannah Louise Shearer; Directed Robert Scheerer

Guest Cast: Matt McCoy; Elizabeth Hoffman; Castulo Guerra; Scott Thomson; Dan Shor; Kevin Peter Hall

56. THE VENGEANCE FACTOR

Written by Sam Rolfe; Directed by Timothy Bond

Guest Cast: Lisa Wilcox; Joey Aresco; Nancy Parsons; Stephen Lee; Mark Lawrence

57. THE DEFECTOR

Written by Ronald D. Moore; Directed by Robert Scheerer

Guest Cast: James Sloyan; Andreas Katsulas; John Hancock

58. THE HUNTED

Written by Robin Bernheim; Directed by Cliff Bole

Guest Cast: Jeff McCarthy; James Cromwell

59. THE HIGH GROUND

Written by Melinda M. Snodgrass; Directed by Gabrielle Beaumont

Guest Cast: Kerrie Keene; Richard Cox

60. DEJA Q

Written by Richard Danus; Directed by Les Landau

Guest Cast: John deLancie; Corbin Berenson

61. A MATTER OF PERSPECTIVE

Written by Ed Zuckerman; Directed by Cliff Boles

Guest Cast: Craig Richard Nelson; Gina Hecht; Mark Margolis

62. YESTERDAY'S ENTERPRISE

Teleplay by Ira Steven Behr, Richard Manning, Hans Beimler and Ronald D. Moore; from a story by Trent Christopher Ganing and Eric A. Stillwell; Directed by David Carson

Guest Cast: Denise Crosby as Tasha Yar; Christopher McDonald; Tricia O'Neil

63. THE OFFSPRING

Written by Rene Echeverria; Directed by Jonathan Frakes

Guest Cast: Hallie Todd; Nicolas Coster

64. SINS OF THE FATHER

Teleplay by Ronald D. Moore and W. Reed Moran; Based on a teleplay by Drew Deighan; Directed by Les Landau

Guest Cast: Charles Cooper; Tony Todd; Patrick Massett; Thelma Lee

65. ALLEGIANCE

Written by Richard Manning and Hans Beimler; Directed by Winrich Kolbe

Guest Cast: Steven Markle; Reiner Schone; Joycelyn O'Brien; Jerry Rector; Jeff Rector

66. CAPTAIN'S HOLIDAY

Written by Ira Steven Behr; Directed by Chip Chalmers

Guest Cast: Jennifer Hetrick; Karen Landry; Michael Champion; Max Grodenchik

67. TIN MAN

Written by Putman Bailey and David Bischoff; Directed by Robert Scheerer

Guest Cast: Harry Groener as Tam; Michael Cavanaugh; Peter Vogt; Colm Meaney

68. HOLLOW PURSUITS

Written by Sally Caves; Directed by Cliff Boles

Guest Cast: Dwight Schultz as Barclay; Charley Lang; Colm Meaney

69. THE MOST TOYS

Written by Shari Goodhartz; Directed by Timothy Bond

Guest Cast: Jane Daly; Nehemiah Persoff; Saul Rubinek

70. SAREK; Television story and teleplay by Peter S. Beagle; From an unpublished story by Mark Cushman and Jake Jacobs; Directed by Les Landau

Guest Cast: Mark Lenard; Joanna Miles; William Denis; Rocco Sisto

71. MÉNAGE À TROI

Written by Fred Bronson and Susan Sackett; Directed by Robert Legato

Guest Cast: Majel Barrett; Frank Corsentino; Ethan Phillips; Peter Slutsken; Rudolph Willrich; Carel Struycken

72. TRANSFIGURATIONS

Written by Rene Echevarria; Directed by Tom Benko

Guest Cast: Mark Lamura; Charles Dennis; Julie Warner

73. THE BEST OF BOTH WORLDS (Part One)

Written by Michael Piller; Directed by Cliff Bole

Guest Cast: Elizabeth Dennehy; George Murdock

SEASON FOUR (1990-91)

74. THE BEST OF BOTH WORLDS (Part Two)

Written by Michael Piller; Directed by Cliff Bole

Guest Cast: Elizabeth Dennehy; George Murdock

75. FAMILY

Written by Ronald D. Moore; Directed by Les Landau

Guest Cast: Jeremy Kemp; Samantha Eggar; Theodore Bikel; Georgia Brown; Dennis Creaghan

76. BROTHERS

Written by Rick Berman; Directed by Rob Bowman

77. SUDDENLY HUMAN

Teleplay by John Whelpley and Jeri Taylor; Story by Ralph Phillips; Directed by Gabrielle Beaumont

Guest Cast: Sherman Howard; Chad Allen; Barbara Townsend

78. REMEMBER ME

Written by Lee Sheldon; Directed by Cliff Bole

Guest Cast: Eric Menyuk; Bill Erwin

79. LEGACY

Written by Joe Menosky; Directed by Robert Scheerer

Guest Cast: Beth Toussaint; Don Mirault

80. REUNION

Teleplay by Thomas Perry and Jo Perry &; Ronald D. Moore and Brandon Braga; Story by Drew Deighan and Thomas Perry and Jo Perry; Directed by Jonathan Frakes

81. FUTURE IMPERFECT

Written by J. Larry Carroll and David Bennett Carren; Directed by Les Landau; Guestcast:; Andreas Katsulas; Chris Demetral; Carolyn McCormick

82. FINAL MISSION

Teleplay by Kacey Arnold-Ince and Jeri Taylor; Story by Kacey Arnold-Ince; Directed by Corey Allen

Guest Cast: Nick Tate

83. THE LOSS

Teleplay by Hilary J. Bader and Alan J. Adler and Vanessa Greene; Story by Hilary J. Bader; Directed by Chip Chalmers

Guest Cast: Kim Braden; Mary Kohnert

84. DATA'S DAY

Teleplay by Harold Apter and Ronald D. Moore; Story by Harold Apter; Directed by Robert Wiemer

Guest Cast: Rosalind Chao; Sierra Pecheur; Alan Scharfe

85. THE WOUNDED

Teleplay by Jeri Taylor; Story by Stuart Charno, Sara Charno and Cy Chernak; Directed by Chip Chalmers

Guest Cast: Bob Gunton; Rosalind Chao; Mark Alaimo; Marco Rodriguez; Time Winters; John Hancock

86. DEVIL'S DUE

Teleplay by Philip Lazebenik; Story by Philip Lazebenik and William Douglas Lansford; Directed by Tom Benko

Guest Cast: Marta Dubois; Paul Lambert; Marcelo Tubert

87. CLUES

Teleplay by Bruce D. Arthurs and Joe Menosky; Story by Bruce D. Arthurs; Directed by Les Landau

Guest Cast: Pamela Winslow; Rhonda Aldrich

88. FIRST CONTACT

Teleplay by Russell Bailey, David Bischoff, Joe Menosky,; Ronald D. Moore and Michael Piller; Story by Marc Scott Zicree; Directed by Cliff Bole

Guest Cast: George Coe; Carolyn Seymour; George Hearn; Michael Ensign; Steven Anderson; Sachi Parker; with Bebe Neuwirth as Lanel

89. GALAXY'S CHILD

Teleplay by Maurice Hurley; Story by Thomas Kartozian; Directed by Winrich Kolbe

Guest Cast: Susan Gibney; Lanei Chapman; Jana Marie Hupp

90. NIGHT TERRORS

Teleplay by Pamela Douglas and Jeri Taylor; Story by Shari Goodhartz; Directed by Les Landau

Guest Cast: Rosalind Chao; John Vickery; Duke Moosekian; Craig Hurley; Brian Tochi; Lanei Chapman

91. IDENTITY CRISIS

Teleplay by Brannon Braga; Based on an unpublished story by Timothy De Haas; Directed by Winrich Kolbe

Guest Cast: Maryann Plunkett; Patti Yasutake; Amick Byram; Dennis Madalone; Mona Grudt

92. THE Nth DEGREE

Written by Joe Menosky; Directed by Robert Legato

Guest Cast: Dwight Schultz; Jim Norton; Kay E. Kuter; Saxon Trainor; Page Leong; David Coburn

93. QPID

Teleplay by Ira Steven Behr; Story by Randee Russell and Ira Steven Behr; Directed by Cliff Bole

Guest Cast: Jennifer Hetrick; Clive Revill; John deLancie

94. THE DRUMHEAD

Written by Jeri Taylor; Directed by Jonathan Frakes

Guest Cast: Jean Simmons as Admiral Satie; Bruce French; Spence Garrett; Henry Woronicz; Earl Billings; Anne Shea

95. HALF A LIFE

Teleplay by Peter Allen Fields; Story by Ted Roberts and Peter Allen Fields; Directed by Les Landau

Guest Cast: David Ogden Stiers as Timicin; Majel Barrett; Michelle Froes; Terrence M. McNally; Carel Struycken

96. THE HOST

Written by Michel Horvat; Directed by Marvin V. Rush

Guest Cast: Franc Luz as Odan; Barabara Tarbuck; Nicole Orth-Pallavicini; William Newman; Patti Tasutake

97. THE MIND'S EYE

Written by Rene Echeverria; Directed by David Livingstone

Guest Cast: Larry Dobkin, John Fleck, Denise Crosby

98. IN THEORY

Written by Joe Menosky and Ronald D. Moore; Directed by Patrick Stewart

Guest Cast: Michele Scarbelli

99. REDEMPTION

Written by Ron Moore; Directed by Cliff Bole

Guest Cast: Robert O'Reilly

Boring, But Necessary Ordering Information!

Payment:
> All orders must be prepaid by check or money order. Do not send cash. All payments must be made in US funds only.

Shipping:
> We offer several methods of shipment for our product. Sometimes a book can be delayed if we are temporarily out of stock. You should note on your order whether you prefer us to ship the book as soon as available or send you a merchandise credit good for other goodies or send you your money back immediately.

Postage is as follows:

Normal Post Office: For books priced under $10.00—for the first book add $2.50. For each additional book under $10.00 add $1.00. (This is per indidividual book priced under $10.00. Not the order total.) For books priced over $10.00—for the first book add $3.25. For each additional book over $10.00 add $2.00.(This is per individual book priced over $10.00, not the order total.)
These orders are filled as quickly as possible. Shipments normally take 2 or 3 weeks, but allow up to 12 weeks for delivery.

Special UPS 2 Day Blue Label Rush Service or Priority Mail(Our Choice). Special service is available for desperate Couch Potatoes. These books are shipped within 24 hours of when we receive the order and should normally take 2 to 3 days to get from us to you.
For the first RUSH SERVICE book under $10.00 add $5.00. For each additional 1 book under $10.00 add $1.75. (This is per individual book priced under $10.00, not the order total.)
For the first RUSH SERVICE book over $10.00 add $7.00 For each additional book over $10.00 add $4.00 per book.(This is per individual book priced over $10.00, not the order total.)

Canadian shipping rates add 20% to the postage total.
Foreign shipping rates add 50% to the postage total.
> All Canadian and foreign orders are shipped either book or printed matter.
> Rush Service is not available.

DISCOUNTS!DISCOUNTS!
> Because your orders keep us in business we offer a discount to people that buy a lot of our books as our way of saying thanks. On orders over $25.00 we give a 5% discount. On orders over $50.00 we give a 10% discount. On orders over $100.00 we give a 15% discount. On orders over over $150.00 we giver a 20 % discount.

Please list alternates when possible.

Please state if you wish a refund or for us to backorder an item if it is not in stock.

100% satisfaction guaranteed.
> We value your support. You will receive a full refund as long as the copy of the book you are not happy with is received back by us in reasonable condition. No questions asked, except we would like to know how we failed you. Refunds and credits are given as soon as we receive back the item you do not want.

Please have mercy on Phyllis and carefully fill out this form in the neatest way you can. Remember, she has to read a lot of them every day and she wants to get it right and keep you happy! You may use a duplicate of this order blank as long as it is clear. Please don't forget to include payment! And remember, we love repeat friends.

COUPON PAGE

_____Secret File: The Unofficial Making Of A Wiseguy $14.95 ISBN # 1-55698-256-9

_____Number Six: The Prisoner Book $14.95   ISBN# 1-55698-158-9

_____Gerry Anderson: Supermarionation $14.95

_____Calling Tracy $14.95 ISBN# 1-55698-241-0

_____How To Draw Art For Comicbooks: Lessons From The Masters
                                                            ISBN# 1-55698-254-2

_____The 25th Anniversary Odd Couple Companion $12.95   ISBN# 1-55698-224-0

_____Growing up in The Sixties: The wonder Years $14.95   ISBN #1-55698-258-5

_____Batmania $14.95   ISBN# 1-55698-252-6

_____The Year Of The Bat $14.95

_____The King Comic Heroes $14.95

_____Its A Bird, Its A Plane $14.95   ISBN# 1-55698-201-1

_____The Green Hornet Book $14.95

_____The Green Hornet Book $16.95 Edition

_____The Unofficial Tale Of Beauty And The Beast $14.95   ISBN# 1-55698-261-5

_____Monsterland Fear Book $14.95

_____Nightmare On Elm Street: The Freddy Krueger Story $14.95

_____Robocop $16.95

_____The Aliens Story $14.95

_____The Dark Shadows Tribute Book $14.95   ISBN#1-55698-234-8

_____Stephen King & Clive Barker: An Illustrated Guide $14.95 ISBN#1-55698-253-4

_____Drug Wars: America fights Back $9.95 ISBN#1-55698-259-3

_____The Films Of Elvis: The Magic Lives On $14.95   ISBN#1-55698-223-2

_____Paul McCartney: 20 Years On His Own $9.95   ISBN#1-55698-263-1

_____Fists Of Fury: The Films Of Bruce Lee $14.95   ISBN# 1-55698-233-X

_____The Secret Of Michael F Fox $14.95   ISBN# 1-55698-232-1

_____The Films Of Eddie Murphy $14.95   ISBN# 1-55698-230-5

_____The Lost In Space Tribute Book $14.95   ISBN# 1-55698-226-7

_____The Lost In Space Technical Manual $14.95

_____Doctor Who: The Pertwee Years $19.95   ISBN#1-55698-212-7

_____Doctor Who: The Baker Years $19.95   ISBN# 1-55698-147-3

_____The Doctor Who Encyclopedia: The Baker Years $19.95   ISBN# 1-55698-160-0

_____The Doctor And The Enterprise $9.95   ISBN# 1-55698-218-6

_____The Phantom Serials $16.95

_____Batman Serials $16.95

MORE COUPON PAGE

_____Batman And Robin Serials $16.95

_____The Complete Batman And Robin Serials $19.95

_____The Green Hornet Serials $16.95

_____The Flash Gordon Serials Part 1 $16.95

_____The Flash Gordon Serials Part 2 $16.95

_____The Shadow Serials $16.95

_____Blackhawk Serials $16.95

_____Serial Adventures $14.95   ISBN#1-55698-236-4

_____Trek: The Lost Years $12.95   ISBN#1-55698-220-8

_____The Trek Encyclopedia $19.95   ISBN#1-55698-205-4

_____The Trek Crew Book $9.95   ISBN#1-55698-257-7

_____The Making Of The Next Generation $14.95   ISBN# 1-55698-219-4

_____The Complete Guide To The Next Generation $19.95

_____The Best Of Enterprise Incidents: The Magazine For Star Trek Fans $9.95

ISBN# 1-55698-231-3

_____The Gunsmoke Years $14.95   ISBN# 1-55698-221-6

_____The Wild Wild West Book $14.95   ISBN# 1-55698-162-7

_____Who Was That Masked Man $14.95   ISBN#1-55698-227-5

NAME:_____

STREET:_____

CITY:_____

STATE:_____

ZIP:_____

TOTAL:_____ SHIPPING_____

SEND TO: Couch Potato, Inc. 5715 N. Balsam Rd., Las Vegas, NV 89130

"The first and only book of It's kind! The story of a new generation of adventures aboard the starship Enterprise. Star Trek fans and film students won't want to miss this one."
—Enterprise Incidents

THE MAKING OF THE NEXT GENERATION

BY EDWARD GROSS

The Making Of The Next Generation
Written by Edward Gross
Pioneer Books and the author of TREK: THE
LOST YEARS, team up again to explore another
untapped aspect of the STAR TREK universe,
with THE MAKING OF THE NEXT GENERA-
TION.
THE MAKING OF THE NEXT GENERATION
provides a behind the scenes look at the first sea-
son of STAR TREK: THE NEXT GENERA-
TION, featuring interviews with cast members Pa-
trick Stewart, Jonathan Frakes, Brent Spiner,
Levar Burton, Denise Crosby, Gates McFadden,
Michael Dorn and Wil Wheaton, a set visit, inter-
views with such crewmembers as directors Paul
Lynch and Joseph Scanlan and writers Dorothy
Fontana, Richard Krzemien and Tracy Torme, as
well as an examination of the metamorphosis that
each script passed through on its journey from
concept to aired episode.
$14.95.............132 pages
ISBN#1-55698-219-4

THE COMPLETE GUIDE
TO THE NEXT GENERATION
By James Van Hise
As the title suggests, this volume is a com-
prehensive guide to the first season of STAR
TREK: THE NEXT GENERATION, providing a
synopsis, critical commentary and credits for ev-
ery episode, from "Encounter at Farpoint" to "The
Neutral Zone". In addition, the text profiles each
of the show's characters and actors that portray
them: Captain Jean Luc Picard/Patrick Stewart,
Commander William Riker/Jonathan Frakes, Doc-
tor Beverly Crusher/Gates McFadden, Counselor
Deanna Troi/Marina Sirtis, Lt. Commander Data/
Brent Spiner, Lt. Geordi LaForge/Levar Burton,
Security Chief Natasha Yar/Denise Crosby, Lt.
Worf/Michael Dorn, Acting-Ensign Wesley
Crusher/Wil Wheaton and the starship Enterprise
itself.
THE COMPLETE GUIDE TO THE NEXT GEN-
ERATION serves as the perfect book for your ref-
erence library. $19.95

A SPECIAL ISSUE OF
FILES MAGAZINE

Next Generation

THE COMPLETE GUIDE

A GUIDE TO EVERY EPISODE

PROFILES OF EVERY CHARACTER

BIOGRAPHIES OF THE STARS

$19.95/$27.95 CANADA

The Trek Crew Book Written by James Van Hise
The crewmembers of the starship Enterprise as presented in the original STAR TREK television series and feature film spin-offs. These fascinating characters, beloved by millions of fans, are the primary reason for the phenomenal on-going success of this Gene Roddenberry created concept.
Never before has a book so completely revealed this ensemble of fine actors, focusing on their careers, examining their unique portrayals of their most famous on-screen alter egos, profiling the characters themselves and presenting in-depth interviews with William Shatner, Leonard Nimoy, DeForest Kelley, James Doohan, George Takei, Walter Koenig and Nichelle Nichols.
Before there was a NEXT GENERATION, there was the original crew and now their story is finally told.
$9.95............108 pages
Painted Cover
ISBN #1-55698-257-7

Couch Potato Inc.   5715 N. Balsam   Las Vegas, NV 89130   (702)658-2090

DOCTOR WHO: THE COMPLETE BAKER YEARS
Written by John Peel

The most popular actor ever to play Doctor Who is Tom Baker. Tom Baker has terrific charisma in the role. He brought the series to America, added millions of new viewers and enchanted audiences.

DOCTOR WHO: THE COMPLETE BAKER YEARS provides summaries and critiques of every Baker episode of the series, profiles Tom Baker as well as the Doctor and the rest of his team; interviews cast members Lalla Ward, Liz Sladen and Louise Jameson, as well as producer Philip Hinchcliffe and writer Bob Baker. Additionally, a special archives section re-presents articles on the Baker Years as they appeared in the British press of the time and a unique index provides easy access to information in the volume.

Fans of Tom Baker, this one's for you! $19.95 ISBN#1-55698-147-3

THE DOCTOR WHO ENCYCLOPEDIA: THE BAKER YEARS
Written by John Peel

This volume contains references for *all* the characters who appeared during the Baker Years, and then examines all of the monsters that have come up against the good doctor in a special section. Want to know who the Trakenites are? Or where the Synge hails from? The answers are all here. THE DOCTOR WHO ENCYCLOPEDIA: THE BAKER YEARS is the perfect companion piece to John Peel's THE TREK ENCYCLOPEDIA.
$19.95 ISBN#1-55698-160-0

"A fine addition to Doctor Who research..."
Fantasy Empire

THE
DOCTOR WHO
ENCYLOPEDIA
THE BAKER YEARS

BY JOHN PEEL

"An essential book for Doctor Who fans..."
Couch Potato

EDITED BY HAL SCHUSTER

THE DOCTOR AND THE ENTERPRISE
Written by Jean Airey

THE DOCTOR AND THE ENTERPRISE is an outrageous satire that combines elements of the aforementioned Traveller of Time and Space with the also aforementioned crew of a certain starship known as Enter....well, you know. Thrown in for good measure is a Wizard of the aforementioned O.Z., a pair of ruby slippers (which just don't shine like they used to), vicious Tin-Woodsmen and more warp outs, beam downs and crack ups than can be described here. Get ready for thrills, excitement and, most of all, plenty of laughs, as famous characters are brought to their most ridiculous extremes.

So kick off your shoes (but watch out for the cat), sit back (still watching out for the cat), put your feet up (but not too high, or you'll screw up your circulation) and enjoy the wild antics of THE DOCTOR AND THE ENTERPRISE. You'll never be the same.
$9.95...........136 pages ISBN#1-55698-218-6 Heavily illustrated

The Lost In Space Tribute Book Written by James Van Hise

LOST IN SPACE remains television's second most popular science fiction series, only falling behind the legendary STAR TREK. The show began in 1965 and ran for five seasons, but has continued to live on in syndication ever since, with legions of fans clamoring for a reunion film.

Now, for the first time ever, Pioneer presents THE LOST IN SPACE TRIBUTE BOOK, the ultimate guide to this unique television series.

Author James Van Hise presents a guide to every episode aired during the series' run, plus exclusive interviews with the late Guy Williams, June Lockhart, Marta Kristen, Mark Goddard, Angela Cartwright, Bill Mumy, the Robot and, of course, Jonathan Harris, as well as various behind-the-scenes personnel. As a special bonus, the book features blueprint reproductions and a guide to the Jupiter 2 spacecraft.

$14.95.........164 pages

Color Cover, Black and White Interior Photographs, Blueprints and Charts

ISBN# 1-55698-226-7